FM 21-10
MCRP 4-11.1D

FIELD HYGIENE
AND SANITATION

**HEADQUARTERS, DEPARTMENT OF THE ARMY
AND COMMANDANT, MARINE CORPS**

A Digireads.com Book
Digireads.com Publishing
16212 Riggs Rd
Stilwell, KS, 66085

Army Field Manual FM 21-10 (Field Hygiene and Sanitation)
By The United States Army
ISBN: 1-4209-2835-X

Please visit *www.digireads.com*

FM 21-10*
MCRP 4-11.1D

HEADQUARTERS
DEPARTMENT OF THE ARMY
AND COMMANDANT, MARINE CORPS
Washington, DC, 21 June 2000

FIELD HYGIENE AND SANITATION

TABLE OF CONTENTS

*This publication supersedes FM 21-10, 22 November 1988.

PREFACE

The purpose of this publication is to assist individual service members, unit commanders, unit leaders, and field sanitation teams (FSTs) in preventing disease and nonbattle injury (DNBI). The publication provides information on preventive medicine measures (PMM) for the individual service member as well as essential information for the unit commander, unit leaders, and the FST on applying unit-level PMM.

When a problem exists beyond unit capabilities, the brigade or division preventive medicine (PVNTMED) section or corps PVNTMED detachments should be called upon to assist in countering the threat.

The use of trade names or trademarks does not constitute endorsement by the Department of Defense (DOD).

Unless this publication states otherwise, masculine nouns and pronouns do not refer exclusively to men.

The proponent of this publication is the United States (US) Army Medical Department Center and School. Submit changes for improving this publication on Department of the Army (DA) Form 2028 and forward it directly to **Commander, US Army Medical Department Center and School, ATTN: MCCS-FCD-L, 1400 East Grayson Street, Fort Sam Houston, Texas 78234-6175.**

CHAPTER 1

INTRODUCTION TO THE MEDICAL THREAT

Section I. MESSAGE TO THE UNIT COMMANDER

DISEASE AND NONBATTLE INJURY

A DNBI casualty can be defined as a military person who is lost to an organization by reason of disease or injury, and who is not a battle casualty. This definition includes persons who are dying of disease or injury due to accidents directly related to the operation or mission to which they were deployed. The acronym, DNBI, does not include service members missing involuntarily because of enemy action or being interned by the enemy (as a prisoner of war). The total number of DNBI casualties is evaluated to identify DNBI rates per number of service members in an operation. The DNBI rates are critical in evaluating the effectiveness of PVNTMED missions within the area of operations (AO) and in determining the health of a force within an operation.

Historically, in every conflict the US has been involved in, only 20 percent of all hospital admissions have been from combat injuries. The other 80 percent have been from DNBI. Excluded from these figures are vast numbers of service members with decreased combat effectiveness due to DNBI not serious enough for hospital admission.

Preventive medicine measures are simple, common sense actions that any service member can perform and every leader must know. The application of PMM can significantly reduce time loss due to DNBI.

How Much Time Does Your Unit Spend Training Service Members on—
Disease and Nonbattle Injury Prevention?
Combat Injury Prevention?

YOUR RESPONSIBILITY

You are responsible for all aspects of health and sanitation of your command. Only you can make command decisions concerning the health of your unit in consideration of the—

- Mission.

- Medical threat.

- Condition of troops.

DO NOT LET THIS HAPPEN TO YOU

Togatabu Island, 1942: The 134th Artillery and the 404th Engineer Battalions were part of a task force preparing to attack Guadalcanal. Fifty-five percent of the engineers and sixty-five percent of the artillerymen contracted a disease called *filariasis* transmitted by mosquitoes. Both units had to be replaced (medically evacuated) without seeing any enemy action because they were not combat ready. The use of insect repellents and insecticides and the elimination of standing water would have prevented this.

Merrill's Marauders: Disease was an important detractor to this famous unit. The medical threat faced by the Marauders in the jungles of Burma was great. Everyone was sick, but some had to stay and fight. Evacuation was limited to those with high fever and severe illness. One entire platoon cut the seats from their pants because severe diarrhea had to be relieved during gunfights. After a bold and successful attack on a major airfield, Merrill's Marauders were so decimated by disease that they were disbanded.

Section II. THE MEDICAL THREAT AND PRINCIPLES OF PREVENTIVE MEDICINE MEASURES

The medical threat is—

- Heat.

- Cold.

- Arthropods and other animals.

- Food- and waterborne diseases.

- Toxic industrial chemicals/materials.

- Noise.

- Nonbattle injury.

- The unfit service member.

PRINCIPLES OF PREVENTIVE MEDICINE MEASURES

- Service members perform individual techniques of PMM.

- Chain of command plans for and enforces PMM.

- Field sanitation teams train service members in PMM and advise the commander and unit leaders on implementation of unit-level PMM.

Failure to Apply the Principles of PMM Can Result in Mission Failure.

CHAPTER 2

INDIVIDUAL PREVENTIVE MEDICINE MEASURES

Section I. HEAT INJURIES

OVERVIEW

Heat injuries can occur anywhere, depending on physical activity (work rate) and clothing worn. However, they occur most frequently during warm-weather training, exposure to high climatic temperatures, high humidity, and bright sunlight. These conditions make it difficult for the body to regulate its temperature. Hot weather also increases daily water requirements, because body water is lost as sweat. Dehydration leads to added heat stress, increased susceptibility to heat injury, reduced work performance, and degraded mission capability.

ACCLIMATIZATION

When the mission permits, all personnel should work and exercise in a manner so that they gradually become acclimatized to the heat and humidity in the AO. Significant heat acclimatization requires at least

3 to 5 days and full acclimatization can take up to 2 weeks. Exercising in the heat and humidity for 1 to 2 hours daily, gradually increasing the workload each day, can produce acclimatization. (Refer to Table 3-1 in Chapter 3.) When the mission does not permit time for gradual increases in workload, then leaders and buddies must observe each other and ensure that everyone drinks plenty of water during each work period. Individuals leaving a cold or cool climate will require additional time to become acclimatized to a hot climate.

DRINK PLENTY OF WATER

Depending on the heat and activity level, you may need to drink from $^1/_2$ to $1^1/_4$ quarts of water per hour—*3 gallons/12 liters per day in hot, dry climates*. **Drinking water is a must in order to prevent heat injury.** If desired, individuals may add flavoring to the water to enhance consumption. Field rations/meal(s), ready to eat (MRE) have flavoring for water in each meal. It the flavoring is used, add it to water in your canteen cup. **Do not** add flavoring to the water in your canteen; it increases the risk of contamination and illness. Never flavor the bulk source water supply. (Flavoring the bulk source water supply will reduce the action of water disinfectants.) See Table 3-1 for water intake requirements.

- Drink extra water **before** starting any mission or hard work. Cool water (60° to 70° Fahrenheit [F]) is absorbed faster than cold water.

- Drink small quantities of cool fluids frequently. Carbohydrate/electrolyte beverages (sport drinks) may provide supplemental nutrients under conditions of extreme calorie and water requirements; such as extremely vigorous activity. However, they cannot replace and must not be used to meet all water requirements.

- Drink "non-caffeinated" fluids even if you are not thirsty. (Caffeine increases water requirements in all environments.)

- Refill your canteens at every opportunity, using only treated water, if possible.

NOTE

The color and volume of the urine steam are good indicators of a service member's hydration status. If your urine stream is **dark yellow** and the volume is small, or if you are constipated and experience hard stools, you may not be drinking enough water. Maintain a urine stream that is **clear or light yellow**. Thirst is not a good indicator of dehydration during physical activity.

USE WORK/REST CYCLES

- Work and rest as your leader directs. (See Table 3-1.) A rest period helps prevent dangerous increases in body temperatures by minimizing heat production.

- Work and rest in the shade, if possible.

EAT ALL MEALS TO REPLACE SALTS

Eating all meals in the field will usually provide the body's requirements for salts. Field rations/MRE meet the daily requirements for minerals and electrolytes (sodium). **DO NOT take extra salt in meals** unless medically indicated.

NOTE

> **DO NOT TAKE SALT TABLETS.** One salt tablet increases your water requirement by at least a pint. Salt draws water from muscles to dilute your blood. Salt tablets can cause vomiting.

RECOGNIZE THE RISK OF MISSION-ORIENTED PROTECTIVE POSTURE/BODY ARMOR/ARMORED VEHICLES

- Mission-oriented protective posture (MOPP)/body armor increases your heat stress. (See Table 3-1.) You must—

  - Drink more water. **DO NOT** EXCEED 1¼ QUARTS PER HOUR.

  - Work and rest as your leader directs.

- You may be at a greater risk of heat injuries when in armored vehicles—you may need to drink more water.

MODIFY YOUR UNIFORM

When directed/authorized by your commander to reduce heat stress and to protect against ultraviolet (UV) radiation, you should—

- Unblouse pants from boots.

- Cover all skin exposed to sun; wear sunscreen and lip balm with a sun protection factor of 15 or higher.

- Protect the eyes from UV with UV-protective sunglasses, especially wraparound sunglasses.

- Seek shade when resting outdoors.

- Keep clothing loose at the neck, wrists, and lower legs.

NOTE

When the threat from biting arthropods is high, keep your shirtsleeves rolled down and pants bloused in boots.

2-5

NOTE

See Graphic Training Aid (GTA) 8-5-50 and FM 21-11, for information on heat injury prevention and first aid.

Section II. COLD INJURIES

OVERVIEW

Cold injuries are most likely to occur when an unprepared individual is exposed to winter temperatures. They can even occur with the proper planning and equipment. The cold weather and the type of operation in which the individual is involved impact on whether a service member is likely to be injured and to what extent. The service member's clothing, physical condition, and mental makeup are also determining factors. Well-disciplined and well-trained service members can be protected, even in the most adverse conditions. Service members and their leaders must know the hazards of exposure to the cold. They must know the importance of personal hygiene, exercise, care of the feet and hands, and the use of protective clothing. Cold injuries may be divided into "freezing and nonfreezing" types. A freezing type is frostbite. The nonfreezing types are chilblains, trench foot, and immersion foot. (See FM 21-11.)

- Frostbite can occur when the temperature is at or near freezing or colder. Frostbite can also occur when the skin is exposed to winds of less than five miles per hour and actual temperature readings of 30° F.

- Trench foot (and immersion foot) results from prolonged exposure to a wet, cold condition, or the outright immersion of the feet in water with a temperature usually below 50° F.

- At the upper range of temperatures, exposure of 12 hours or more will cause injury. Shorter duration at or near 32° F will cause the same injury.

- A trench foot injury is usually associated with immobilization of the feet.

WEAR UNIFORM PROPERLY

- Wear the clothing your commander and leaders direct.

- Wear clothing in loose layers (top and bottom). Avoid tight clothing, including tight underwear.

- Keep clothing clean and dry. Remove or loosen excess clothing when working or in heated areas to prevent sweating.

- Wear headgear to prevent body heat loss. The body loses large amounts of heat through the head.

- Avoid spilling fuel or other liquids on clothing or skin. Evaporating liquids increase heat loss and cool the skin. Also, liquid stains on clothing will reduce the clothing's protective effects.

- Change wet/damp clothes as soon as possible. Wet/damp clothing pulls heat from body.

KEEP YOUR BODY WARM

- Keep moving, if possible.

- Exercise your big muscles (arms, shoulders, trunk, and legs) frequently to keep warm.

- If you must remain in a small area, exercise your toes, feet, fingers, and hands.

- Avoid the use of alcohol as it makes your body lose heat faster.

- Avoid standing directly on cold, wet ground, when possible.

- Avoid tobacco products. The use of tobacco products decreases blood flow to your skin.

- Eat all meals to maintain energy.

- Drink plenty of water and/or warm nonalcoholic fluids. Dark yellow urine means you are not drinking enough fluids! You can dehydrate in cold climates too!

- Buddies should monitor each other for cold weather injury.

PROTECT YOUR FEET

- Bring several pairs of issue boot socks with you.

- Keep socks clean and dry. Change wet or damp socks as soon as possible. Socks can become wet from sweating. Apply foot powder on feet and in boots when changing socks.

- Wash your feet daily, if possible.

- Avoid tight socks and boots (completely lace boots up as loosely as possible).

- Wear overshoes to keep boots dry.

NOTE

A decrease in physical activity reduces the exposure **time necessary to produce injury.** In all types of footgear, feet perspire more and are generally less well ventilated than other parts of the body. Moisture accumulates in socks, decreasing their insulating quality. The feet are susceptible to cold injury and are less frequently observed than the remainder of the body.

PROTECT YOUR HANDS

- Wear gloves with inserts, or mittens with inserts.

- Warm hands under clothing if they become numb.

- Avoid skin contact with snow, fuel, or bare metal.

- Waterproof gloves by treating with waterproofing compounds, such as snow seal.

PROTECT YOUR FACE AND EARS

- Cover your face and ears with a scarf or other material, if available.

- Wear your insulated cap with flaps down or wear a balaclava and secure under your chin.

- Warm your face and ears by covering them with your hands. **Do not rub face** and ears.

- Do not use face camouflage when windchill is -10° F or below; prevents detection of cold weather injury (frostbite).

NOTE

Rubbing cold extremities can be potentially harmful. Frostbitten areas that are rubbed can cause additional injury to the affected areas.

- Wear sunscreen. Solar UV exposure is doubled when you are surrounded by snow.

- Exercise facial muscles.

PROTECT YOUR EYES

- Wear sunglasses (or goggles) (Sun, Wind, and Dust, National Stock Number [NSN] 8465-01-004-2893) to prevent snow blindness (gray lens insert for above system is NSN 8465-01-004-2891).

- Wear Spectacles, Protective, Laser-Ballistic, NSN 8465-01-416-4626, or Special Protective Eyewear, Cylindrical System, NSN 8465-01-416-4626.

- Improvised sunglasses (slit goggles), if actual sunglasses are not available, can be made from the field rations/MRE cardboard box or other opaque material.

PROTECT YOUR BUDDY

- Watch for signs of frostbite on the service member's exposed skin. The affected skin will appear as pale/gray/waxy areas (it may be hard to see these changes in poor lighting or on service members with dark skin).

- Ask the service member if his feet, hands, ears, or face are numb and need rewarming.

- **DO NOT** allow the service member to sleep directly on the ground.

- To prevent carbon monoxide poisoning—

    - **DO NOT** let the service member sleep in or near the exhaust of a vehicle with the engine running.

    - **DO NOT** let the service member sleep in an enclosed area where an open fire is burning

NOTE

Service members may check circulation in the fingers and the toes by pinching the nail beds and checking how fast the color returns in the beds under the nails. The slower the return to a natural color, the more serious the potential for frostbite on the fingers and the toes.

NOTE

See GTA 8-6-12 and FM 21-11 for information on cold injury first aid procedures. During extended activities in a cold environment, warming areas should be provided; for example, a service member performing guard duty.

Section III. ARTHROPODS AND OTHER ANIMALS OF MEDICAL IMPORTANCE

OVERVIEW

Poor sanitation and improper waste disposal under wartime conditions greatly increase the disease vector potential of such common pests as filth flies and rodents. Even in mobile field situations these "camp followers" have historically amplified sanitation problems, often resulting in epidemics of diarrheal diseases that have caused many casualties. This threat is even greater in urban areas converted to temporary or semipermanent military use. A dangerous temptation in field training or in deployment operations is to ignore the field sanitation standards. Some people think, "The rules don't apply here." Yielding to that temptation can cost your health and the health of those around you. There is no excuse for forgetting to bring protective equipment or failing to use it. Be sure to follow all safety precautions on all labels of the pesticides that you use. They are there for a reason—to protect your health.

USE THE DEPARTMENT OF DEFENSE INSECT/ARTHROPOD REPELLENTS

The concurrent use of a skin insect repellent (N, N-diethyl-M-toluamide [DEET], NSN 6840-01-284-3982) and a clothing insect repellent (permethrin [NSN 6840-01-278-1336 and 6840-01-345-0237]) is necessary to obtain maximum protection against insects/arthropods.

APPLY N, N-DIETHYL-M-TOLUAMIDE

- Apply DEET insect repellent to all exposed skin.

- Follow label directions.

- Apply a light, even coating to exposed skin, not under clothing.

- **DO NOT** apply to the eyes and lips, or to damaged skin.

- One application may last 8 to 12 hours; if you receive bites, reapply a light uniform coating of repellent.

- Application of DEET can be safely used with camouflage face paint. Apply a thin layer of DEET first, then apply face paint.

NOTE

Reapplication of DEET may be necessary (check container label) due to heavy sweating, or after river-crossing operations, exposure to rain, or in locations where arthropod density is very high.

APPLY PERMETHRIN CLOTHING REPELLENTS TO FIELD UNIFORMS/ SLEEPING EQUIPMENT

- Permethrin is the most effective clothing repellent available.

- Treat military field uniforms, including Nomex®/Kevlar uniforms, tent liners, ground cloths, and bed nets with permethrin. This should be done before wearing in field training or military operations. **Follow label instructions when applying to clothing**.

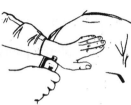

- Permethrin will remain in the material after repeated washings.

- Treated uniforms can be safely worn in the rain or when crossing rivers or streams.

NOTE

Permethrin does not rinse out in cold water (or rain or streams).

- **DO NOT** apply directly to skin, to underwear, or to cap.

- **DO NOT** wear treated uniforms unless they are first thoroughly dried after treating.

- **Apply permethrin outdoors or in well-ventilated areas only.**

2-15

- Wear uniform as your commander directs.

- Wear a loose fitting uniform, not tightly tailored, to prevent arthropods from biting through the fabric; repair tears/holes.

- When the arthropod threat is high—

  - Blouse pants in boots and completely lace boots.

  - Tuck undershirt in at waist.

  - Wear sleeves down.

  - Button blouse/shirt at the neck and wrist.

  - Do not use aftershave lotion, cologne, or perfumed deodorants or soaps in the field; they attract arthropods.

  - Wear headgear (cap, helmet, arthropod head net) when necessary to protect your head.

KEEP YOUR BODY AND UNIFORM CLEAN

- Bathe every day if possible, or at least once a week. Good personal hygiene practices reduce infestation of insects such as body lice and mites.

- Wash your uniform frequently (a minimum of every 7 days) to remove arthropods and their eggs which may be attached to the uniform. If the situation permits, use the quartermaster laundry; otherwise, use a stream, lake, or washbasin. Air-dry uniforms, especially underwear and socks, if possible.

FOLLOW MEDICAL ADVICE

- Take medications that help prevent diseases (such as anti-malaria pills) when directed by your commander.

- Use medications, such as cream/shampoo, when prescribed by medical personnel for treatment of lice, chiggers, poison ivy, and so forth.

PROTECT YOURSELF AT NIGHT

- Ensure your bed net is in good repair.

- Use your bed net when sleeping.

- Tuck net under sleeping pad or sleeping bag so there are no openings.

- Follow the label directions and precautions when using DOD-approved insect spray (for example, Insecticide, Aerosol d-PHENOTHRIN, 2%) if insects are present inside the bed net (and inside closed tent). Allow vapors to disperse for 10 minutes before entering the enclosure.

- Treat bed net with permethrin for added protection.

- Repair holes in your bed net. Generously apply DEET skin repellent to those areas likely to touch the insect net during sleep (knees, hands, elbows, and feet) to prevent bites through holes in the fabric.

PROTECT YOURSELF FROM OTHER MEDICALLY IMPORTANT ARTHROPODS AND ANIMALS

Spiders, Scorpions, and Centipedes—

- Remove spiders from tents or buildings.

- Shake out and inspect clothing, shoes, and bedding before use.

- Eliminate collections of papers, unused boxes, scrap lumber, and metal.

- Thoroughly clean beneath and behind large items; spiders and scorpions may be resting in these areas.

- Check field latrines before use; run a small stick under the rim of the latrine hole to dislodge any spiders or scorpions there. Spiders and scorpions may rest under toilet seat or inside latrine box.

- Wear gloves when handling paper, cloth, lumber, or other items that have been stored for long periods.

- Check around rocks and logs before resting against them.

- Use a long-handled tool or stick to turn over debris before removing it.

- Remove accumulations of boards, rocks, and other debris to eliminate the resting/ hiding areas of spiders and scorpions.

- Wear leather gloves to remove rocks, lumber, and such from the ground.

NOTE

In many locations worldwide, centipedes are more of a problem than scorpions, but the PMM are the same for both pests.

Snakes—

- Do not handle, play with, or disturb snakes or other wildlife.

- Avoid swimming in areas where snakes abound.

- Keep hands off rock ledges where snakes may be hiding or sunning.

- Look over the area before sitting down, especially if in deep grass or among rocks.

- If snakes are known to inhabit the area, sleep off the ground, if possible.

- If military situation permits, avoid walking about an area during the period from dusk to complete daylight, as many snakes are active during this period.

- Avoid camping near piles of brush, rocks, or other debris.

- Never step over large rocks or logs without first checking to see what is on the other side.

- Turn rocks and logs toward you when they have to be removed so you will be shielded should snakes be beneath them.

- Handle freshly killed snakes only with a long-handled tool or stick; snakes can inflict fatal bites by reflex action after their death.

NOTE

If bitten, try to kill the snake and bring its head with you to the medical treatment facility. If you cannot bring the snake's head with you, get an accurate description of the snake to assist medical personnel in treating you. **DO NOT panic!**

DOMESTIC AND WILD ANIMALS OR BIRDS

- **Do not** handle or approach so-called "pets."

- Exclude such animals from your work and living areas, unless cleared by veterinary personnel.

- **Do not** collect or support (feed or shelter) stray or domestic animals/birds in the unit area, unless cleared by veterinary personnel.

Section IV. POISONOUS PLANTS AND TOXIC FRUITS

OVERVIEW

Many poisonous plants have thorns that can puncture the skin, introduce poison into the skin, or cause infection. (See FM 21-76.) Clothing can serve as a protective barrier for the skin. Clothing can also be a source of exposure if it is not properly cleaned after contact with poisonous plants. Toxic fruits can also cause significant harm to service members, ranging from minor wounds to rapidly fatal poisoning. The threat is magnified for US military personnel who may be unfamiliar with native species and unaware of these poisonous plants and toxic fruits.

- Avoid contact with poisonous plants by properly wearing the uniform.

- Avoid areas where poisonous plants grow.

- Only eat plants or parts of plants that have been approved. If you do not know, **DO NOT** eat it.

- **DO NOT** put grasses or woody twigs or stems in your mouth; they may be poisonous.

Section V. FOOD-/WATER-/WASTEBORNE DISEASE/ILLNESS

OVERVIEW

Prior to deployment, the key to preventing illnesses and diseases from consumption of food and water is following the strict guidelines and procedures established by PVNTMED. During deployments, apply individual PMM. Infectious diarrhea results from contamination of water and food by bacteria, viruses, and parasites. Water- and foodborne diarrheal diseases are of particular concern to the military because they can be spread to large numbers of service members simultaneously with disastrous consequences for combat readiness. Parasites (amoebas, Giardia, and tapeworms) consumed in water or undercooked food, especially meat and fish, can cause prolonged illness. Diarrhea, especially when vomiting or fever is present, can cause dehydration.

WATER

Fill your canteen with treated water at every chance. When treated water is not available, you must disinfect the water in your canteen using one of the following methods.

Preferred method—iodine tablets:

- Fill your canteen with the cleanest water available.

- Put two iodine tablets in the canteen of water. Double these amounts in the 2-quart canteen.

- Place cap on canteen. Shake canteen to dissolve tablets. Wait 5 minutes. Loosen the cap and tip the canteen over to allow leakage around the canteen threads. Tighten the cap and wait an additional 25 minutes before drinking.

2-23

Alternate methods—

Chlorine Ampules:

- Fill your canteen with the cleanest water available.

- Mix one ampule of chlorine with one-half canteen cup of water; stir the mixture with a clean device until contents are fully dissolved.

- Pour one canteen capful of the above solution into your canteen of water.

- Place the cap on your canteen and shake. Slightly loosen the cap and tip the canteen over to allow leakage around threads. Tighten cap and wait 30 minutes before drinking.

- If the nuclear, biological, and chemical (NBC) canteen cap is used, then use two caps of the solution.

NOTE

By wearing gloves or wrapping the ampule in paper or cloth, you can avoid cutting your hands when breaking open the glass ampule.

Emergency Water Treatment Kit (CHLOR-FLOC® Tablets):

- Tear off the top of the plastic water treatment bag at the perforation (first time use).

- Fill the treatment bag one-half full with the cleanest water available; add 1 tablet.

- Fold bag tightly three times and fold tabs in.

- Hold bag firmly and shake until tablet dissolves. Swirl 10 seconds. Let the bag sit for 4 minutes. Swirl again for 10 seconds.

- Let bag sit for an additional 15 minutes.

- Insert filter pouch in neck of canteen. Pour water from bag through the filter into the canteen. Avoid pouring sediment into the filter.

- Rinse the filter with treated water after use. Always filter through the same side of the filter.

- Rinse sediment from treatment bag. Save bag for water treatment only.

```
                          CAUTION

  Do not drink from the treatment bag!  The water is still contaminated
  and must be filtered before drinking.  Not filtering may cause
  stomach and intestinal disorders.
```

Household Bleach:

NOTE

Ensure bleach is unscented. (To check for chlorine residual, see Tasks 7 and 8, Appendix A.)

- Fill your canteen with the cleanest water possible.

- Read the label on the bleach bottle to determine amount of available chlorine. Liquid chlorine laundry bleach usually has about 5 to 6 percent available chlorine. Based upon the strength of the household bleach, add the chlorine to the canteen as directed in Table 2-1.

Table 2-1. Drops of Household Bleach to be Added to a One-Quart Canteen

AVAILABLE CHLORINE	CLEAR WATER	COLD OR CLOUDY WATER
1 PERCENT	10	20
4—6 PERCENT	2	4
7—10 PERCENT	1	2

- Place the cap on your canteen and shake. Slightly loosen the cap and tip the canteen over to allow leakage around threads. Tighten the cap and wait 30 minutes before drinking the water.

BOILING

- When chlorine or iodine is not available, bring water to a rolling boil for 5 minutes.

- In an emergency, boiling water for just 15 seconds will help. Boiled water must be protected from recontamination.

CAUTION

If water is suspected of NBC contamination, do not attempt to treat. Seek a quartermaster water supply.

FOOD

- Do not buy foods, drinks, or ice from civilian vendors unless approved by veterinary personnel or PVNTMED personnel.

2-27

CAUTION

Obtain food from approved sources ONLY.

- In emergency situations, choose low-risk foods such as baked goods (breads) and thick-skinned fruits that you can peel before eating. Eat only fruits and vegetables that grow above the ground.

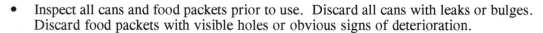

- When eating in local establishments or from approved vendors, only eat hot food entrees or raw foods that you can wash and peel prior to eating.

- Inspect all cans and food packets prior to use. Discard all cans with leaks or bulges. Discard food packets with visible holes or obvious signs of deterioration.

- Do not eat foods or drink beverages that have been prepared in galvanized containers (*zinc poisoning*). Canned, bottled, or vacuum-packed products should draw in air when opened (suction/hissing sound). If no sound is heard, or if there are any off-odors, colors, or foaming (except for carbonated beverages), discard the product. Do not taste.

- Do not eat or drink local (unapproved) ice, snow cones, open drinks with ice, or similar products; such food can cause foodborne illness/disease.

WASH YOUR HANDS

Use soap and drinking (potable) water—

- After using the latrine.

- Before touching eating utensils or food.

- After eating.

- After handling any item that can potentially transfer germs.

- Frequently during the work day to keep your hands free of germs.

WASH YOUR MESS KIT/EATING UTENSILS

A sure way to get diarrhea is to use a dirty mess kit or eating utensils. Protect yourself by washing your mess kit/eating utensils—

- In a mess kit laundry/sanitation center.

- With treated water or disinfectant solution.

DISPOSE OF YOUR WASTE IN AN APPROVED MANNER

On a march, personal disposal bags should be used first, if available. If not available, personal cat holes can be used only if your unit is on the move! Always dispose of your waste immediately if your unit is on the move to prevent flies from spreading germs from waste to your food. Disposing of your waste also helps keep unwanted animals out of your bivouac area. Chemical toilets or burnouts are to be used in bivouac area. (See Chapter 3, Section V.)

Section VI. PERSONAL HYGIENE AND PHYSICAL AND MENTAL FITNESS

OVERVIEW

Physically fit, well-trained, and well-led service members can succeed under the harshest circumstances.

KEEP PHYSICALLY FIT

- Physically fit service members are less likely to get sick or injured.

- Use caution when exercising in extremely hot or cold weather; heat/cold injuries can occur. Actively participating in physical fitness training assists you in becoming acclimatized to the field environment.

NOTE

See FM 21-20 for more information on physical fitness training.

PREVENT SKIN INFECTIONS

Bathe frequently; if showers or baths are not available, use a washcloth daily to wash—

- Your genital area.

- Your armpits.

- Your feet.

- Other areas where you sweat or that become wet, such as between thighs, (or for females, under the breasts) and between buttocks.

Keep skin dry.

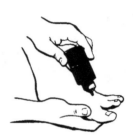

- Use foot powder on your feet, especially if you have had fungal infections on your feet in the past.

- Use talcum powder in areas where wetness is a problem (such as between the thighs, and for females, under the breasts).

Wear proper clothing.

- Wear loose fitting uniforms; they allow for better ventilation. Tight fitting uniforms reduce blood circulation and ventilation.

- Do not wear nylon or silk-type undergarments in hot or humid environments.

PREPARE FOR THE FIELD

- All service members need to bring toilet articles such as soap, shampoo, washcloths, towels, toothbrush, dental floss and fluoride toothpaste, and talcum powder and foot powder, with them. **Do not share these items** to prevent the spreading of infections.

- Males need a razor and blades. Females need sanitary napkins or tampons.

Remember, during a deployment, you may not be able to easily obtain these items if you run out; bring at least a 2-month supply.

PREVENT DENTAL DISEASE

Tooth decay and gum infections can cause severe illness if not prevented or treated early.

- Brush teeth and gums after meals, or at least once a day. Use fluoride toothpaste. If toothpaste is not available, brush without it.

- Use dental floss at least once a day.

- Rinse your mouth with potable water after brushing and flossing; also, rinse frequently during the day when drinking water.

- Remember, consuming sugary food and drink requires more frequent cleaning of teeth and gums.

PREVENT GENITAL AND URINARY TRACT INFECTIONS

For males:

- Wash the head of your penis when washing your genitals. If uncircumcised, pull the foreskin back before washing.

- Protect yourself from sexually transmitted diseases (STD). Avoid sexual contact or use a condom; condoms reduce the chance of STD transmission.

For females:

- Wash your genital area daily.

- Do not use perfumed soaps or feminine deodorants in the field; they cause irritation and attract arthropods.

- Protect yourself from STD. Avoid sexual contact, or at least insist that your sex partner uses a condom—condoms help prevent STD transmission.

- **DO NOT** douche unless directed by medical personnel.

- **DO NOT** wear nylon or silk undergarments; cotton undergarments are more absorbent and allow the skin to dry.

NOTE

Some individuals do not drink enough fluids and tend to hold their urine due to a lack of privacy in the field. Urinary tract infections are one of the most frequent medical problems females face in the field. Drinking extra fluids and urinating more often will help prevent these infections.

SLEEP WHEN YOU CAN

- Follow your leaders' instructions and share tasks with buddies so everyone gets some time to sleep safely.

- Sleep whenever possible.

  - Take catnaps as the mission allows, but expect to need a few minutes to fully wake up.

  - Sleep as much as you can *before* going on a mission that may prevent sleep.

  - Learn and practice techniques to relax yourself quickly.

NOTE

Only sleep in safe and/or designated areas. Never sleep in parked vehicles while the motor is running.

MEASURES AGAINST THE EFFECTS OF SLEEP LOSS

Protect against the temporary effects of sleep loss on alertness, mood, and task performance.

- Take short stretch breaks or get light exercise in place.

- **Do not trust your memory; write things down.** Get into the habit of writing things down that you must remember (except crucial details that might compromise the mission if they were lost or captured). Double-check your communications and calculations.

- Watch out for your mind playing tricks (seeing things that are not there) when very tired; check strange observations before acting.

IMPROVE RESISTANCE TO STRESS

- Fear and physical signs or symptoms of stress are normal reactions before and during combat or other dangerous/life-threatening situations. You should not let fear or stress keep you from doing your job.

- Talk about what is happening with your buddies, especially during after-action debriefings.

- Learn ways to relax quickly.

- Integrate new replacements into your group and get to know them quickly.

- If you must join a new group, be active in establishing friendships.

- Give each other moral support.

- Care for your buddies and work together to provide everyone food, water, sleep, and shelter, and to protect against heat, cold, poor sanitation, and enemy action.

NOTE

See FM 21-11 for first-aid procedures for stress reactions.

Section VII. NOISE

OVERVIEW

If you have to raise your voice to be understood, it is too noisy. Put on hearing protectors. The use of hearing protective devices will enhance hearing and comprehension in the presence of a hazardous noise.

PROTECT YOURSELF AND YOUR MISSION FROM NOISE

- Wear properly fitted earplugs. Different types include single flange, triple flange, and hand formed.

- Use vehicle headgear such as a helicopter crew helmet, an armor crew helmet, or earmuffs.

- Keep earplugs and earmuffs clean to prevent ear infections.

- Avoid noise or limit time around noise to only critical tasks.

Section VIII. TOXIC INDUSTRIAL CHEMICALS/MATERIALS

OVERVIEW

Consider risk management in planning all operations; identify potential sources of danger or mission hazards that can be anticipated in performing a mission. Always weigh the risks and benefits and establish controls to reduce unnecessary hazards.

RECOGNIZE AND PREPARE FOR TOXIC INDUSTRIAL CHEMICALS/ MATERIAL THREATS

Occupational hazards.

- Exhaust from engines and fuel space heaters.

- Gases from weapons firing, such as rockets and M8 smoke.

NOTE

When using M8 smoke in training or operations, follow unit standing operating procedures (SOPs) and leaders and controller's instructions for use of protective masks and for moving through smoky areas, especially in buildings and tunnels.

- Solvents used to clean weapons.

- Greases and oil from vehicle maintenance repair.

- Detergents used to clean equipment.

Industrial hazards.

- Compressed gases.

- Industrial solvents.

- Hazardous chemical waste.

- Materials used at water treatment plants.

- Materials and water used at waste sewage and water treatment plants.

Biological/radiological hazards.

- Medical waste.

- Materials used at medical research facilities.

- Radioactive isotopes.

- Substances at nuclear power plants.

- Depleted uranium.

RECOGNIZE THE INJURY

- Carbon monoxide is colorless, odorless, and tasteless. It causes headache, sleepiness, coma, and death.

- Hydrogen chloride is a very irritating gas that reacts with water (body fluids) to produce hydrochloric acid in the throat, lungs, and eyes. It causes coughing, tissue acid burns, and flu-like lung disease.

- M8 smoke is a very irritating gas. It can cause severe coughing, wheezing, and lung damage, if inhaled.

- Bore/gun gases cause the same effects as carbon monoxide and hydrogen chloride.

- Solvents, greases, and oils cause skin rashes, burns, drying, and infections. They cause damage to the liver, blood, and brain. Also, many are poisons that may cause cancer.

- Medical waste causes disease.

- Radioactive materials cause radiation illness.

PROTECT YOURSELF AND YOUR MISSION FROM TOXIC INDUSTRIAL CHEMICALS/ MATERIALS

NOTE

Service members should always be aware that material safety data sheets (MSDS) accompany stores of toxic chemicals when units are deployed, and they serve as an immediate reference in cases of exposure or injury. Once a unit is deployed and set up, these MSDS should be kept as part of the unit's SOP when handling the specified chemicals/materials.

Carbon monoxide.

- Run engines outdoors or with shop doors/windows open.

- Keep sleeping area windows slightly open where you sleep for ventilation and air movement.

- **DO NOT** sleep in vehicles with the engine running or use engine exhaust for heat.

- **DO NOT** park vehicles near air intakes to tents, trailers, or environmental control units.

Bore/gun gases.

- Use onboard vehicle ventilation systems.

- Keep bore evacuator well maintained.

- Try to keep some air movement in gun emplacements or in protected batteries.

Solvents, greases, and oils.

- Use "safety" Stoddard solvent.

- Never substitute one solvent for a "better" one; for example, never use benzene or fuel in place of Stoddard.

- Wear coveralls, if available, and rubber gloves.

- Wash or change clothing often, especially when soiled by chemicals or fuel.

- Always follow label instructions for use and safety precautions.

- Use ventilation systems in areas where fumes are present or when conditions and materials dictate.

Biological waste.

- Always use disposable rubber gloves when working with biological materials.

- Wear coveralls/rubberized aprons, as necessary.

- Wear goggles or safety glasses, as necessary.

- Wear facemasks and air-filtered breathing masks approved for specific tasks, as necessary, when removing/working with biological waste.

- Dispose of biological waste materials according to unit SOPs and product label instructions.

CHAPTER 3

LEADERS' PREVENTIVE MEDICINE MEASURES

NOTE

In addition to the specific measures that follow, leaders must remember and apply the principle that the most effective PMM they can apply is to visibly set the example in the use of all the individual PMM that are discussed throughout this FM.

Section I. HEAT INJURIES

PLAN FOR THE HEAT

- Maximize physical fitness and heat acclimatization before deployment.

- Use your FST to train individuals and their leaders in PMM against heat.

- Acclimatize personnel to high temperatures as gradually as the mission will allow.

- Brief service members on dangers of sunburn and skin rashes and the importance of good personal field hygiene.

- Obtain weather forecast for time/area of training/mission.

- Ensure adequate supplies of potable water are available (up to 3 gallons per day per service member just for drinking) (See Table 3-1). Issue a second canteen to service members in hot weather operations. In the desert, additional canteens may be required.

- Know the location of water distribution points.

- Set up a buddy system to maximize rehydration and minimize heat injuries.

- Ensure medical support is available for treatment of heat injuries.

- Plan the placement of leaders to observe for and react to heat injuries in dispersed training (road marches), or operational missions.

- If the mission permits, plan to—

    - Train during the cooler morning hours.

- Serve heavy meals in the evening, rather than at noon.

OBTAIN AND USE HEAT CONDITION INFORMATION

- Obtain heat condition information per your unit's SOP or contact the local supporting PVNTMED detachment or section. Heat condition may be reported as--

  - Category: 1, 2, 3, 4, and/or 5.

  - Wet bulb globe temperature (WBGT) index.

- Use heat condition information to determine required water intake and work/rest cycles (Table 3-1).

NOTE

Training by lecture or demonstration, maintenance procedures on equipment, or personal hygiene activities (such as skin and foot care) can be performed during rest periods.

Table 3-1. Fluid Replacement Guidelines for Warm Weather Training
(Applies to Average Acclimated Service Member Wearing Hot Weather Uniform)

HEAT CATEGORY	WBGT INDEX DEGREES F	EASY WORK		MODERATE WORK		HARD WORK	
		WORK/ REST MIN	WATER INTAKE QT/HR	WORK/ REST MIN	WATER INTAKE QT/HR	WORK/ REST MIN	WATER INTAKE QT/HR
1	78-81.9	NL	$1/2$	NL	$3/4$	40/20	$3/4$
2 (GREEN)	82-84.9	NL	$1/2$	50/10	$3/4$	30/30	1
3 (YELLOW)	85-87.9	NL	$3/4$	40/20	$3/4$	30/30	1
4 (RED)	88-89.9	NL	$3/4$	30/30	$3/4$	20/40	1
5 (BLACK)	> 90	50/10	1	20/40	1	10/50	1

The work/rest times and fluid replacement volumes will sustain performance and hydration for at least 4 hours of work in the specified heat category. Individual water needs will vary ± $1/4$ quart/hour.
NL= no limit to work time per hour.
Rest means minimal physical activity (sitting or standing) accomplished in shade, if possible.
CAUTION: Hourly fluid intake should not exceed 1 $1/4$ quarts.
Daily fluid intake **should not exceed 12 liters.**
Wearing body armor adds **5° F** to WBGT Index.
Wearing all MOPP overgarments adds **10° F** to WBGT Index.

Table 3-1. Fluid Replacement Guidelines for Warm Weather Training (Continued)
(Applies to Average Acclimated Service Member Wearing Hot Weather Uniform)

EASY WORK	MODERATE WORK	HARD WORK
WEAPON MAINTENANCE WALKING HARD SURFACE AT 2.5 MPH, ≤ 30 LB LOAD GUARD DUTY MARKSMANSHIP TRAINING DRILL AND CEREMONY	WALKING LOOSE SAND AT 2.5 MPH, NO LOAD WALKING HARD SURFACE AT 3.5 MPH, ≤ 40 LB LOAD CALISTHENICS PATROLLING INDIVIDUAL MOVEMENT TECHNIQUES, SUCH AS LOW CRAWL, HIGH CRAWL DEFENSIVE POSITION CONSTRUCTION	WALKING HARD SURFACE AT 3.5 MPH, ≥ 40 LB LOAD WALKING ON LOOSE SAND AT 2.5 MPH WITH LOAD FIELD ASSAULTS

WARNING

Hourly fluid intake should not exceed 1¼ quarts. Daily fluid intake should not exceed 12 liters.

ENFORCE INDIVIDUAL PREVENTIVE MEDICINE MEASURES

Leaders must—

- Enforce water intake by—

  - Observing service members drinking required amounts. Encourage frequent drinking of water in small amounts.

  - Ensuring that service members practice good field hygiene.

  - Providing cool water; if desired, you can add flavoring after disinfection to enhance consumption. Personnel should use their canteen cup for consumption of flavored water. **DO NOT add flavoring to canteen water; use only plain water in canteen.**

  - Ensuring troops drink water before starting any hard work or mission (in the morning, with/after meals).

  - Ensuring buddy system is being used.

  - Frequently checking service members' canteens for water; not beverages.

- Making sure service members have adequate time to eat and drink as mission permits. Permit personnel to consume carbohydrate/electrolyte beverages (sports drinks) as supplemental nutrients under conditions of extreme calorie and water requirements; such as extremely vigorous activities.

- Reduce heat injuries by—

    - Enforcing work/rest cycles when the mission permits. Permitting personnel to work/rest in the shade, if possible.

    - Encouraging service members to eat all meals for needed salts.

    - Adjusting workload to size of individuals, when possible.

    - Be prepared for heat casualties and decreased performance when water and work/rest cycle recommendations cannot be met.

MODIFY WEAR OF THE UNIFORM

Direct/authorize service members to—

- Keep skin covered while in sun.

- Keep uniform loose at neck, wrists, and lower legs (unblouse pants).

NOTE

If the medical threat from biting arthropods is high, keep sleeves rolled down and pants bloused in boots.

IDENTIFY SPECIAL CONSIDERATIONS

Identify and modify training/physical activity for service members with high-risk conditions of heat injuries, such as—

- Diseases/injuries, especially fevers, vomiting, diarrhea, heat rash, or sunburn.

- Use of alcohol within the last 24 hours.

- Overweight/unfit.

- Over 40 years old.

- Fatigue/lack of sleep.

- Taking medication (especially for high blood pressure, colds, or diarrhea).

- Previous heatstroke/severe heat exhaustion.

- Lack of recent experience in a hot environment.

Section II. COLD INJURIES

PLAN FOR THE COLD

- Use your FST to train individuals and their leaders in PMM against cold.

- Obtain weather forecast for time/area of training/mission.

- Ensure the following are available as the tactical situation permits:

  - Covered vehicles for troop transport, if tactical situation permits.

  - Cold weather clothing.

  - Laundry services.

  - Warming tents/areas.

  - Hot rations/hot beverages.

  - Drinking water.

- Inspect service members (before starting training/mission) to ensure—

  - Availability, proper fit, and wear of cold weather gear.

- Clean, dry, proper-fitting clothing.

- Each service member has several pairs of socks, depending on the nature and duration of the mission.

- Frequently rotate guards or other service members performing inactive duties.

- Ensure medical support is available for treatment should cold weather injuries occur.

DETERMINE AND USE WINDCHILL FACTOR

- Obtain temperature and wind speed information as directed by your unit's SOP or contact the local supporting PVNTMED detachment or section.

- Calculate windchill from Table 3-2.

NOTE

Cold injuries can and do occur in nonfreezing temperatures. Hypothermia can occur in mildly cool weather.

Table 3-2. Windchill Chart

ESTIMATED WIND SPEED (IN MPH)	ACTUAL TEMPERATURE READING (°F)											
	50	40	30	20	10	0	-10	-20	-30	-40	-50	-60
	EQUIVALENT CHILL TEMPERATURE (°F)											
CALM	50	40	30	20	10	0	-10	-20	-30	-40	-50	-60
5	48	37	27	16	6	-5	-15	-26	-36	-47	-57	-68
10	40	28	16	4	-9	-24	-33	-46	-58	-70	-83	-95
15	36	22	9	-5	-18	-32	-45	-58	-72	-85	-99	-112
20	32	18	4	-10	-25	-39	-53	-67	-82	-96	-110	-121
25	30	16	0	-15	-29	-44	-59	-74	-88	-104	-118	-133
30	28	13	-2	-18	-33	-48	-63	-79	-94	-109	-125	-140
35	27	11	-4	-20	-35	-51	-67	-82	-98	-113	-129	-145
40	26	10	-6	-21	-37	-53	-69	-85	-100	-116	-132	-148

(WIND SPEEDS GREATER THAN 40 MPH HAVE LITTLE ADDITIONAL EFFECT.)

LITTLE DANGER IN LESS THAN ONE HOUR WITH DRY SKIN. MAXIMUM DANGER OF FALSE SENSE OF SECURITY.

INCREASING DANGER DANGER FROM FREEZING OF EXPOSED FLESH WITHIN ONE MINUTE.

GREAT DANGER FLESH MAY FREEZE WITHIN 30 SECONDS.

NOTE: 1. TRENCH FOOT AND IMMERSION FOOT MAY OCCUR AT ANY POINT ON THIS CHART.
2. F = 9/5 C + 32.

Table 3-3. Windchill Categories (See Windchill Table)

WORK INTENSITY	LITTLE DANGER	INCREASED DANGER	GREAT DANGER
HIGH DIGGING FOXHOLE, RUNNING, MARCHING WITH RUCKSACK, MAKING OR BREAKING BIVOUAC	INDIVIDUALS OR SMALL UNIT LEADERS: BLACK GLOVES OPTIONAL; MANDATORY BELOW 0 DEGREES F; INCREASED HYDRATION.	INCREASED SURVEILLANCE BY EXTREME COLD WEATHER SYSTEM OR EQUIVALENT; MITTENS WITH LINERS; NO FACIAL CAMOUFLAGE; EXPOSED SKIN COVERED AND KEPT DRY; REST IN WARM, DRY, SHELTERED AREA; COLD WEATHER, VAPOR BARRIER BOOTS BELOW 0 DEGREES F.	POSTPONE NON-ESSENTIAL ACTIVITY; ESSENTIAL TASKS ONLY WITH LESS THAN 15 MINUTES EXPOSURE; COVER ALL SKIN.
LOW WALKING, MARCHING WITHOUT RUCKSACK, DRILL AND CEREMONY	INCREASED SURVEILLANCE; COVER EXPOSED FLESH WHEN POSSIBLE; MITTENS WITH LINERS AND NO FACIAL CAMOUFLAGE BELOW 10 DEGREES F; FULL HEAD COVER BELOW 0 DEGREES F; KEEP SKIN DRY, ESPECIALLY AROUND NOSE AND MOUTH.	RESTRICT NONESSENTIAL ACTIVITY; 30-40 MINUTE WORK CYCLES WITH FREQUENT SUPERVISORY SURVEILLANCE FOR ESSENTIAL TASKS (SEE ABOVE).	CANCEL OUTDOOR ACTIVITY, IF POSSIBLE.
SEDENTARY SENTRY DUTY, EATING, RESTING, SLEEPING, CLERICAL WORK	SEE ABOVE; FULL HEAD COVER AND NO FACIAL CAMOUFLAGE BELOW 10 DEGREES F; COLD WEATHER, VAPOR BARRIER BOOTS BELOW 0 DEGREES F; SHORTEN DUTY CYCLES; PROVIDE WARMING.	POSTPONE NONESSENTIAL ACTIVITY; 15-20 MINUTE WORK CYCLES FOR ESSENTIAL TASKS; WORK GROUPS OF NO LESS THAN 2 PERSONNEL; NO EXPOSED SKIN.	CANCEL OUTDOOR ACTIVITY, IF POSSIBLE.

These guidelines are generalized for worldwide use. Commanders of units with extensive extreme cold weather training and specialized equipment may opt to use less conservative guidelines.

- Then use Table 3-4 to apply PMM guidance:

Table 3-4. Windchill Preventive Medicine Measures

WINDCHILL	PREVENTIVE MEDICINE MEASURES
30° F AND BELOW	ALERT PERSONNEL TO THE POTENTIAL FOR COLD INJURIES.
25° F AND BELOW	LEADERS INSPECT PERSONNEL FOR WEAR OF COLD WEATHER CLOTHING. PROVIDE WARM-UP TENTS/AREAS/HOT BEVERAGES.
0° F AND BELOW	LEADERS INSPECT PERSONNEL FOR COLD INJURIES. INCREASE THE FREQUENCY OF GUARD ROTATIONS TO WARMING AREAS. DISCOURAGE SMOKING.
-10° F AND BELOW	INITIATE THE BUDDY SYSTEM—HAVE PERSONNEL CHECK EACH OTHER FOR COLD INJURIES.
-20° F AND BELOW	MODIFY OR CURTAIL ALL BUT MISSION-ESSENTIAL FIELD OPERATIONS.

- The windchill index gives the equivalent temperature of the cooling power of wind on exposed flesh.

  - Any movement of air has the same effect as wind (running, riding in open vehicles, or helicopter downwash).

  - Any dry clothing (mittens, scarves, masks) or material which reduces wind exposure will help protect the covered skin.

- Trench foot injuries can occur at any point on the windchill chart and—

  - Are much more likely to occur than frostbite at "LITTLE DANGER" windchill temperatures, especially on extended exercises/missions and/or in wet environments.

  - Can lead to permanent disability, just like frostbite.

IDENTIFY SPECIAL CONSIDERATIONS

- Conditions that place service members at high risk of cold injuries include—

  - Previous trench foot or frostbite.

- Fatigue.

- Use of alcohol.

- Significant injuries.

- Poor nutrition.

- Use of medications that cause drowsiness.

- Little previous experience in cold weather.

- Immobilized or subject to greatly reduced activity.

- Service members wearing wet clothing.

- Sleep deprivation.

- Identify the special hazards of carbon monoxide poisoning and fire that may affect your cold weather operations.

ENFORCE INDIVIDUAL PREVENTIVE MEDICINE MEASURES

- Ensure service members wear clean and dry uniforms in loose layers.

- Ensure service members remove outer layer(s) before starting hard work or when in heated areas (before sweating).

- Have service members inspect their socks and feet at least daily when operating in cold and/or wet environments.

- Ensure service members to—

  - Wash their feet daily.

  - Wear clean and dry socks.

  - Use warming areas when available.

  - Eat all meals to ensure sufficient calories are consumed to maintain body heat.

  - Drink plenty of water and/or nonalcoholic fluids. In cold weather, fluid intake is often neglected, leading to dehydration.

  - Exercise their big muscles or at least their toes, feet, fingers, and hands to keep warm.

- Institute the buddy system in cold weather operations. Service members taking care of each other decrease cold injuries.

Section III. ARTHROPODS AND OTHER ANIMALS OF MEDICAL IMPORTANCE

PLAN FOR THE ARTHROPOD, RODENT, AND OTHER ANIMAL THREAT

- Obtain information on biting and stinging arthropods and other animals (such as snakes, domestic and wild animals, or birds) which could be a threat—

    - Through unit medical channels from the command PVNTMED representative.

    - From the health service support (HSS) annex to operation plan/order.

- Use your FST—

    - Train your service members in PMM.

    - Control insects and other medically important arthropods in your AO.

    - Control rodents and other medically important animals in your AO.

    - Remind service members to avoid handling insects, arthropods, snakes, and other animals to prevent bites or injury. Animals that appear to be healthy may transmit rabies and other zoonotic diseases.

- Keep personnel from eating in sleeping/work areas; prevent attracting insects, rodents, and other animals.

- Animal mascots should not be kept or maintained unless cleared by veterinary personnel.

- Ensure that—

  - Each service member has a bed net in good repair and treated with permethrin repellent.

  - Immunizations are current. Prophylaxis (for example, anti-malaria tablets) is available for issue as required.

  - Laundry and bathing facilities are available.

  - Field sanitation team supplies and equipment are available and can be replenished.

- Request assistance from a PVNTMED unit (through medical or command channels) when control of biting arthropods, rodents, or other animals is beyond the capabilities of your unit.

ENFORCE INDIVIDUAL PREVENTIVE MEDICINE MEASURES

- Ensure all uniforms are impregnated with permethrin before field training or deployment.

- Ensure each service member has DOD skin (DEET) and clothing (permethrin) insect repellent and uses them. However, cooks, other food handlers, and kitchen police personnel must not use repellent on their hands when preparing and serving food, or when cleaning food service utensils, dishes, and food serving areas.

- Direct service members to keep—

  - Shirts buttoned.

  - Sleeves rolled down.

  - Pants bloused inside boots.

- Ensure service members—

  - Bathe/shower regularly (field expedients will do); a field shower or bath with a clean change of uniform should be accomplished once each week to control body lice.

  - Discontinue the use of aftershave lotions, colognes, perfumes, and scented soaps; they attract insects.

  - Use permethrin treated bed nets and the DOD-approved aerosol insect (Insecticide, d-Phenothrin, 2%, Aerosol, NSN 6840-01-412-4634); spray inside the net if necessary.

- Observe service members taking anti-malaria pills or other prophylaxis (when prescribed by the medics).

- Use your FST to identify suspected lice infestations and refer for medical treatment.

MINIMIZE EXPOSURE TO ARTHROPOD, RODENT, AND ANIMAL THREAT

- If the mission permits—

  - Use your FST to assist you in selecting bivouac sites.

  - Occupy areas distant from insect/arthropod breeding areas such as natural bodies of water.

  - Avoid areas with high grass or dense vegetation.

  - Use FST recommendations and assistance in applying pesticides for area control around living areas and in natural bodies of water.

  - Drain or fill in temporary standing water sites in occupied area (empty cans, used tires, or wheel ruts after rains).

  - Clear vegetation in and around occupied area.

- Maintain area sanitation by enforcing good sanitation practices.

  - Properly dispose of all waste.

  - Protect all food supplies.

  - Police area regularly.

  - Exclude pests (rats, mice, lice, and flies).

NOTE

See Appendix A for performance of tasks relating to PMM against arthropods and rodents.

Section IV. POISONOUS PLANTS AND TOXIC FRUITS

- Obtain information on poisonous plants and toxic fruits that could be a threat—

  - Through unit medical channels from the command PVNTMED representative.

  - From the HSS annex to operation plan/order.

- Use your FST to—

    - Train your service members in PMM.

    - Display and provide information on the kinds of dangerous plants and fruits in the unit area.

- Enforce individual PMM by—

    - Proper wearing of the uniform.

    - Avoidance of poisonous plants where possible.

    - Avoidance of consuming potentially dangerous vegetation and fruits.

    - Avoidance of putting grasses and twigs in the mouth.

Section V. FOOD-/WATER-/WASTEBORNE DISEASE/ILLNESS

PLAN FOR SAFE WATER

- Know the location of approved water distribution points.

- Make sure your unit has an adequate supply of—

    - Iodine water purification tablets (1 bottle for each individual).

    - Field chlorination kits.

    - Bulk chlorine.

    - Chlor-Floc® kits.

- Ensure water trailers and tankers (400 gallon and above) are inspected by PVNTMED personnel semiannually.

- Inspect water containers before use.

- Check the residual chlorine of bulk water supplies (5-gallon cans, water pillows, water trailer) before drinking and at least daily thereafter. (See Tasks 7 and 8, Appendix A.)

PLAN FOR SAFE FOOD

- Ensure food service personnel maintain foods at safe temperatures.

- Inspect food service personnel daily and refer for medical evaluation those with illness and/or skin infections.

- Make sure foods, drinks, and ice purchased from civilian vendors are approved by the command medical authority.

- Supervise the use of the mess kit laundry/sanitation center.

- Ensure food service personnel and service members use handwashing devices.

- Ensure all food waste is transported to an approved disposal site, buried, or burned daily (at least 30 meters from food preparation area and water source).

PLAN FOR THE CONSTRUCTION AND MAINTENANCE OF FIELD SANITATION DEVICES

- Determine type of field waste disposal devices required.

  - The primary type of human waste disposal devices in bivouac areas are the chemical toilets. Individual waste collection bags are the primary type used when on the march.

  - The type of improvised waste disposal used will depend on the mission, length of stay in the area, terrain, and weather conditions. When chemical toilets are not available, the burn-out latrine is the preferred improvised waste disposal device.

NOTE

Always check local, state, federal, or host-nation regulations for restrictions or prohibitions on using standard or improvised field devices and waste disposal in the field.

- Select locations for field latrines.

  - As far from food operations as possible (100 meters or more). Downwind and down slope, if possible.

  - Down slope from wells, springs, streams, and other water sources (30 meters or more).

- Set up, construct, and maintain latrines (see Task 9, Appendix A, for requirements).

  - As soon as the unit moves into a new area, detail service members to set up chemical toilets or dig latrines. (See previous **NOTE**.)

  - Detail service members to clean latrines daily.

  - Instruct the FST to spray the latrines with insecticide as necessary (not the pit contents).

  - Always provide handwashing facilities at the food service facilities and the latrines. Make use of handwashing devices at latrines mandatory.

- Cover, transport, burn, or bury waste daily.

- Use the FST to train service members and unit leaders in PMM against food-/water-/wasteborne diseases.

NOTE

See Appendix A for performance of tasks relating to PMM against food-/water-/wasteborne diseases.

Section VI. PERSONAL HYGIENE AND PHYSICAL AND MENTAL FITNESS

KEEP YOUR UNIT PHYSICALLY FIT

- Ensure that leaders at all levels recognize the benefits of physical fitness. Leaders must be role models, leading by example.

- Take a positive approach to physical fitness with service members. A physically fit service member is less likely to be a combat loss from disease or injury.

NOTE

See FM 21-20 for more information.

PLAN FOR PERSONAL HYGIENE

- Provide shower/bathing facilities in the field. All personnel must bathe at least once a week and have a clean change of clothing to reduce the health hazard associated with body lice.

- Inspect service members' personal equipment to ensure they have sufficient personal hygiene supplies—soap, washcloths, towels, a toothbrush, dental floss, fluoride toothpaste, and razor and razor blades (females should have sanitary napkins or tampons).

  - Ensure undergarments are cotton (not silk, nylon, or polyester).

  - Ensure uniforms fit properly (not tight).

  - Ensure service members have several pairs of issue boot socks; the number will depend on the type and length of the mission.

- Use your FST to train your service members in personal hygiene.

- Ensure service members receive annual dental examinations and needed oral health care. Make sure all oral health appointments are kept. Use low operational requirement periods to ensure all personnel maintain a good oral health status.

ENFORCE SLEEP DISCIPLINE

- The mission, unit readiness, and individual security must come first, but never miss a chance to give everyone in the unit time to sleep.

- When feasible, set work/rest shifts.

- Do not allow service members to sleep in areas where they may be run over by vehicles, or in other unsafe areas.

- During *continuous operations*, set shifts and rotate jobs to allow everyone at least 3 to 4 hours uninterrupted sleep per 24-hour period.

- During brief (up to 48 hours) sustained operations when shifts are impossible, rotate jobs so all individuals catnap as safely and comfortably as possible. The loss of sleep will reduce the service member's ability to perform his duties and the leader's ability to make decisions.

NOTE

Ensure that sleeping individuals observe safety precautions. Use ground guides for vehicles in bivouac areas.

ENFORCE PREVENTIVE MEDICINE MEASURES FOR THE EFFECTS OF SLEEP LOSS

- Those individuals with the most complex mental or decision-making jobs need the most sleep. This means you and your most critical leaders and operators!

- Cross train individuals to perform the critical tasks and delegate limited authority among leaders, thus enabling all to get necessary rest.

ENSURE WELFARE, SAFETY, AND HEALTH OF UNIT

- Ensure the best and safest water, food, equipment, shelter, sanitation, and sleep possible are provided.

- Educate service members to maintain professional pride and personal caring for themselves, each other, and their equipment.

- Know the personal backgrounds and the military skills of your service members. Chat with them informally about themselves. Be attentive and understanding while listening to service members.

- Utilize group support and counsel for service members with *home front* problems.

- Assign jobs to maintain a balance between having qualified people in key positions while sharing the load, hardship, and risks fairly.

- Use challenging and difficult environments during training to increase your own and the unit's coping skills and confidence.

REDUCE UNCERTAINTY BY KEEPING EVERYONE INFORMED

- Brief unit personnel on the situation, objectives, and conditions that the mission or environment may involve.

- Explain reasons for hardships, delays, and changes.

- Do not give false reassurances. Prepare your service members for the worst and put any unexpected challenges or reversals in a positive perspective.

- Deal with rumors firmly and honestly. Prevent the spread of rumors.

- Make contingency plans and follow SOP to reduce the effects of surprise.

PROMOTE COHESION WITHIN THE UNIT

- Use equipment drills, physical fitness training, team sports, and field *stress training* to stimulate mutual reliance and closeness.

- Bring unit members together for meals, award ceremonies, and other special occasions.

- Integrate new members by assigning sponsors and ensuring rapid familiarization.

IMPART UNIT PRIDE

- Educate service members in the history and tradition of the small unit, its parent units, and the branch of Service.

- Honor the historical examples of initiative, endurance, and resilience, of overcoming heavy odds, and of self-sacrifice.

Section VII. NOISE

PLAN FOR NOISE

- Identify existing noise in your unit. If necessary, request PVNTMED assistance in identifying sources.

- Ensure that hearing conservation is part of the unit SOP.

- Ensure all service members are medically fitted for hearing protectors and are issued multiple sets.

- Ensure all service members have annual hearing test/screening.

- Control noise sources.

  - Isolate by distance; that is, keep troops away from noise, if possible.

  - Isolate by barrier; for example, use sandbags.

  - Use organic equipment controls; for example, keep mufflers and engine covers in good repair.

- Train unit to do mission while wearing hearing protectors.

- Post **Noise Hazard** signs in noise hazardous areas and on noise hazardous equipment.

ENFORCE INDIVIDUAL PROTECTIVE MEASURES

Ensure that service members—

- Wear earplugs or other hearing protective devices.

- Do not remove inserts from aircraft or tracked vehicle helmets.

- Avoid unnecessary exposure.

- Limit necessary exposure to short, infrequent, mission-essential times.

- Clean their hearing protectors.

PROTECT MISSION

- Be aware of short-term noise effects on the service member's ability to hear combat significant noise.

- Assign listening post (LP)/observation post (OP) to troops least affected by noise,augment LP/OP with night vision devices and/or increase the number of audible alarms around your position.

Section VIII. TOXIC INDUSTRIAL CHEMICALS/MATERIALS

PLAN FOR CHEMICALS

- Identify sources of toxic industrial chemicals/materials in your unit. If necessary, request PVNTMED assistance in identifying sources.

- Obtain safer chemicals for unit operations, if available.

- Observe cautions/warnings posted in technical manuals dealing with solvents corrosives, and other hazardous materials. (Refer to MSDS that accompany stores of toxic chemicals/materials.)

ENFORCE INDIVIDUAL PREVENTIVE MEDICINE MEASURES

Ensure that service members—

- Repair engines outside or vent engine exhaust to outside.

- Keep their sleeping quarters ventilated.

- Do not use vehicle engines as heaters.

- Use/maintain onboard ventilation systems.

- Are trained and drilled to self-protect themselves around hydrogen chloride and M8 smoke.

- Maintain bore/gun gas evacuation systems.

- Use "safety" Stoddard solvent.

- Have adequate clean gloves, coveralls, and other protective gear.

- Follow label instructions on chemical containers.

CHAPTER 4

UNIT FIELD SANITATION TEAM

FIELD SANITATION TEAM CONCEPT

- During World War II, it became apparent that more action was needed at the unit level to counter the medical threat. (Remember Togatabu Island and the jungles of Burma? [pages 1-2 and 1-3]) To answer this need, the FST concept was developed.

- Selected members from each company-sized unit were designated to receive special training in DNBI prevention so they could advise the commander in PMM for DNBIs. This training enabled the unit commander to provide arthropod control, individual and unit disinfection of water, and safe food supplies. This resulted in commanders being able to reduce DNBI losses.

SCOPE OF FIELD SANITATION TEAM OPERATIONS

The FST—

- Conducts arthropod and rodent control operations in the field as directed by the commander. In garrison, the FST is in a training status. During mobilization, the FST performs its field sanitation duties.

- Ensures that unit leaders are supervising the disinfection of unit water supplies. Instructs the troops in methods of individual water purification.

- Assists the commander by inspecting food service operations.

- Monitors the waste disposal procedures and the construction of garbage and soakage pits; and then inspects these devices for proper waste disposal procedures use.

- Ensures personnel have individual waste collection bags and the unit's chemical toilets are set up and operated correctly. Monitors disposal methods of individual bags and chemical toilet contents. Monitors the construction of field latrines and urinals when chemical toilets are not available. Inspects these devices for proper sanitation.

- Provides unit training in the use of individual PMM.

- Applies pesticides as required/necessary for the control of arthropods.

FIELD SANITATION TEAM TASKS

Unit FSTs serve as advisors to the commander on individual and unit PMM that prevent DNBI. To assess the medical threat (disease/illness risk), the team members must be able to perform the following tasks:

- Inspect water containers and trailers.

- Disinfect unit water supplies.

- Check unit water supply for chlorine.

- Inspect unit field food service operations.

- Inspect unit waste disposal operations.

- Control arthropods, rodents, and other animals in unit area.

- Train unit personnel in use of individual PMM.

- Monitor status of PMM in unit.

- Assist in selection of a unit bivouac site.

- Supervise the construction of field sanitation devices.

- Monitor unit personnel in the application of individual PPM.

NOTE

All unit leaders should be able to perform these tasks.

SELECTION OF PERSONNEL

Selection of personnel for the unit FST should be based on the following:

- Units having organic medical personnel (combat medics) *WILL* use them as the FST.

- When organic medical personnel are not available, selected team members should be personnel whose normal field duties allow them to devote time to field sanitation activities.

- At least one member must be a noncommissioned officer when organic medical personnel are not available.

TRAINING

Members of the FST are required to receive training in basic sanitation techniques, disease control, and individual PMM. Training includes—

- Use of insect repellents, uniform impregnants, and protective clothing.

- Use and repair of screening and bed nets.

- Use of residual and space insecticide sprays.

- Rodent control measures.

- Food service sanitation.

- Unit waste disposal procedures.

- Water purification procedures, to include determination of chlorine residual.

- Personal hygiene.

- Heat/cold injury prevention, to include WBGT determination and use of the windchill chart.

- Other subjects as they relate to the medical threat in the unit's AO, to include noise hazards and hearing protection.

HOW TO MAKE YOUR FIELD SANITATION TEAM THE BEST IN THE COMMAND

- Select soldiers you can rely on.

- After they are trained, use them during—

  - Service training and evaluation programs.

  - Field training exercises.

- Unit training on PMM.

- Predeployment training on the medical threat in the deployment AO.

- Ensure your unit has a functional FST SOP.

NOTE

Do not let your FST just be an Inspector General requirement. Make it an asset you can use. Your FST has a critical role and can assist you in protecting the health of unit personnel.

APPENDIX A

UNIT-LEVEL PREVENTIVE MEDICINE MEASURES TASKS

TASK 1: Control biting insects.

EQUIPMENT NEEDED: 1-gallon or 2-gallon sprayer, ready-to-use insecticide, and individual repellents (DEET and permethrin).

STEPS OF PERFORMANCE:

MOSQUITOES:

STEP 1: Identify common mosquito-breeding areas:

- Mosquito landing counts and trapping.

- Standing water.

- Artificial water containers.

STEP 2: Control:

- If possible, drain standing water.

- Empty artificial water containers.

- Avoid setting up bivouac sites near mosquito-breeding areas.

- Enforce individual use of DOD insect repellent systems (DEET on skin and permethrin on uniforms and bed nets).

- Have FST spray pesticide on adult mosquito-resting areas using 1-gallon or 2-gallon sprayer (see Task 2), if necessary.

FLEAS:

STEP 1: Identify rodent infestations or the presence of wild or domestic cats and dogs in the unit area (rodents, cats, and dogs carry fleas).

STEP 2: Control:

- Have service members in unit use individual DOD insect repellents.

- Exclude rodents and other wild animals from camps and buildings.

- Have FST spray pesticide, using 1-gallon or 2-gallon sprayer (see Task 2) around rodent burrows and harborage.

- **DO NOT** allow service members to keep "pet" animals.

LICE:

STEP 1: Identify lice infestation:

- Head lice—look for lice and eggs attached to the hair, close to the scalp. Eggs are attached directly to the hairs.

- Crab lice—usually associated with the pubic area (groin), but can be found attached to other body hairs. The eggs are attached directly to the hair.

- Body lice—generally found in the seams of infested persons' clothing. The eggs are attached to the fibers of the garments. Body lice tend to move to the body of the host only during the actual feeding process.

STEP 2: Control:

- Refer individuals with lice infestation for medical treatment.

- Enforce high standards of personal hygiene. Require frequent showering and laundering of bedding and clothing (once a week at a minimum).

- To prevent body lice, enforce individual use of permethrin-treated battle dress uniform/cammies.

- Avoid sexual contact (for crab lice).

TICKS AND MITES:

STEP 1: Identify tick- or mite-infested areas—

- Grassy areas.

- Animal trails or resting areas.

- Rodent burrows.

STEP 2: Control:

- Avoid walking through tick-infested areas.

- Cut down vegetation in and around camps.

- Enforce individual use of DOD insect repellent.

- If necessary, have FST spray area with pesticide, using 1-gallon or 2-gallon sprayer to apply pesticide (see Task 2).

- Enforce a buddy system where troops perform checks not only on themselves but on their buddy as well. If ticks are found—

  • Remove any attached ticks promptly and carefully without crushing, using gentle steady traction with forceps (tweezers) close to the skin to avoid leaving mouthparts in the skin;

  • Protect hands with gloves, cloth or tissue when removing ticks from humans or animals;

  • Ensure that the body of the tick is not separated from its head.

NOTE

Lyme disease, Rocky Mountain spotted fever, ehrlichiosis, and encephalitis can be contracted through tick bites. Beware of ticks when passing through the thick vegetation they may cling to. When cleaning host animals for food, or when gathering natural materials to construct a shelter, you must be on the lookout for them. Buddy checks are important. If diagnosed early, the diseases mentioned above can be cured. If not, they can lead to death.

BITING FLIES:

STEP 1: Identify problems with biting flies and their breading sites.

- Moist soil near ponds and stream banks.

- Decaying vegetation and animal manure.

- Rodent burrows, rock walls, and cracks in walls of buildings.

STEP 2: Control:

- Enforce use of DOD insect/arthropod repellents (DEET on the skin and permethrin on uniforms.

- Avoid areas with biting fly problems or breeding sites.

FILTH FLIES:

STEP 1: Identify infestations and breeding areas, such as—

- Open latrines.

- Uncovered food and waste.

- Ground soaked with liquid kitchen waste or food scraps on wet soil.

- Animal barnyards near AO.

STEP 2: Control:

- Remove, cover, or burn latrine waste.

- Keep food and waste covered.

- Use fly swatters for small to moderate numbers of filth flies. Only use the DOD-approved aerosol (Insecticide, d-Phenothrin, 2%, 12 ounce Aerosol, NSN 6840-01-412-4634) pesticide if large numbers of flies are in an enclosed area (do not use in food service operations).

- Ensure proper disposal of waste collection bags.

- Have FST use a 1-gallon or 2-gallon sprayer to spray pesticide on ground that is wet with kitchen waste, in field latrines, and on fly-resting sites (see Task 2).

- Use toxic fly baits.

COCKROACHES:

STEP 1: Identify cockroach infestations and breeding areas, such as—

- Food service areas.

- Latrines/shower facilities.

- Trash collection points.

STEP 2: Control:

- Enforce good sanitation practices.

- Ensure proper collection and removal of food waste.

- Have FST use a 1-gallon or 2-gallon sprayer to spray pesticide as spot treatment in food service areas and as a residual spray to outside surfaces of buildings and trash collection points.

SPIDERS:

STEP 1: Identify infestations of medically important spiders (black widow, tarantula, and brown recluse spider).

NOTE

Use caution when entering into and clearing out of old, infrequently used buildings.

STEP 2: Control:

- Eliminate unnecessary rubbish and other debris in the bivouac area.

- Have FST use a 1-gallon or 2-gallon sprayer (see Task 2) to spray around tents, field latrines, or other spider habitats.

SCORPIONS and CENTIPEDES:

STEP 1: Identify places where scorpions and centipedes are a problem.

- Rocky areas.

- Inside of building.

- Tents.

STEP 2: Control:

- Have FST use a 1-gallon or 2-gallon sprayer (see Task 2) on nesting sites around the entire tent or other structure, forming a band 2-feet high from the ground level.

- Saturate all cracks and crevices with insecticide.

BEES, WASPS, AND ANTS:

STEP 1: Identify places where these insects are a problem. Locate the nests.

STEP 2: Control:

- Educate troops to avoid nests.

- Have FST use a 1-gallon or 2-gallon sprayer (see Task 2) on the nesting sites. Use caution to avoid stings from disturbed insects. If the task is too great or too dangerous, contact PVNTMED personnel for assistance.

TASK 2: Use the 1-gallon or 2-gallon compressed air sprayer.

EQUIPMENT NEEDED: 1-gallon or 2-gallon sprayer and authorized insecticide, respirator, gloves, nonvented goggles, and other personal protective equipment, as appropriate.

NOTE

Only personnel certified as DOD Pesticide Applicator may apply pesticides. Uncertified persons may apply pesticides if they are properly trained by and under the direct supervision of a certified pesticide applicator.

STEPS OF PERFORMANCE:

STEP 1: Determine the job to be done (pest, area to be treated, and pesticide type).

STEP 2: Assemble the compressed air sprayer. Select the correct nozzle and attach to the end of the wand, fill the tank half full of clean water, and pressurize the tank to ensure that the tank and nozzle are operational. Pressurize to approximately 40 to 60 pounds per square inch (psi) of pressure. If the sprayer does not have a gauge, approximately 30 to 35 pump strokes will usually be sufficient. Squeeze the handle on the wand to check nozzle performance. If the sprayer is operational, release pressure from tank. If the sprayer leaks, replace the gaskets or tighten the connections on the hose, wand, and nozzle.

STEP 3: Read the insecticide label.

- Always read the label before doing anything.

- Always follow all instructions on the label. **The label is the law.**

CAUTION

Wear chemical resistant gloves during mixing and spraying. Gloves, Chemical and Oil Protective, NSN 8415-01-012-9294 (size 9) or NSN 8415-01-013-7832 (size 10) are recommended. Wear an approved pesticide respirator, if required by the label. DO NOT use the NBC protective mask when applying pesticides. Avoid skin contact with insecticide.

STEP 4: Add pesticide to the clean water in the sprayer tank. Finish filling the sprayer with clean water to the appropriate level. **DO NOT fill the sprayer to the top.** Leave space for pumping air pressure into the tank. Put the pump assembly into the sprayer and tighten.

STEP 5: Pump the sprayer.

- Pump the sprayer 30 to 35 times to achieve 40 to 60 psi pressure.

- There should be a slight resistance to pumping when this pressure is achieved. **DO NOT** over pump.

STEP 6: Spray insecticide.

- Point nozzle at area to be sprayed and squeeze the handle on the wand.

- Continue spraying until area is covered.

NOTE

Record all pesticide applications. The record should include location of application, name of pesticide used, and amount of pesticide used. Pesticide applications must be reported to higher echelon command, using **Department of Defense Form 1532-1** as required by **DOD Instruction 4150.7.**

STEP 7: Clean the sprayer.

- Clean the sprayer with soap and water, then flush the tank at least 3 times with clear water.

- Rinse all parts in clear water.

- Reassemble and spray clear water through nozzle. If the sprayer is not cleaned after use, vital parts will corrode.

STEP 8: Store cleaned sprayer.

- Turn the sprayer tank upside down with pump assembly separated to keep tank dry.

CAUTION

Always wash your hands and chemical resistant gloves, respirator, goggles, and other personal protective equipment with soap and water after spraying. Store personal protective equipment away from pesticides and applicator.

TASK 3: Control domestic rodents.

EQUIPMENT NEEDED: Tamper-proof rodent bait stations, rat snap trap (mechanical spring), mouse snap trap (mechanical spring), and rodenticides.

STEPS OF PERFORMANCE:

STEP 1: Identify rodent infestations and breeding and harborage areas, such as—

- Underground burrows.

- Around building foundations.

- Under rubbish piles.

- Near food sources.

STEP 2: Control:

- Enforce food sanitation practices, such as eliminating garbage and food waste in the bivouac area and keeping all food and waste covered.

- Locate trash dumps away from sleeping/berthing and food service areas.

- Clear all possible nesting areas by removing unnecessary rubbish and other debris.

- Modify buildings and structures to prevent rodents from having easy access.

• Use rodent snap traps and poison baits simultaneously for effective control. Poison baits must be placed in tamper/spill-proof containers with bilingual labels (English and local). Read the label and wear chemical resistant gloves when handling poison baits.

CAUTION

Wear chemical resistant gloves while handling rodenticides. Avoid skin contact with rodenticides. Wear plastic gloves when handling dead rodents. Place dead rodents in plastic bags; seal and dispose of the bags in landfills, or incinerate.

TASK 4: Prevent injuries due to venomous snakebite.

STEPS OF PERFORMANCE:

STEP 1: Be familiar with venomous snakes in the AO and with areas where snakes may be a problem.

• Rocky areas.

• Areas with rodent infestations.

• Heavy vegetation.

STEP 2: Control:

- Be familiar with field treatment of snakebites.

- Educate personnel on avoiding snakes and preventing snakebites.

- Prevent and control rodents (food sources for snakes) around camps and bivouac sites.

- Exclude snakes from buildings.

TASK 5: Inspect unit food service operations.

EQUIPMENT NEEDED: Thermometer, Self-Indicating Bimetallic, 0° F to 220° F, NSN 6685-00-444-6500. Clipboard with writing material.

BACKGROUND INFORMATION:

Some foods support the rapid growth of disease organisms that cause diarrhea; these foods are called:

POTENTIALLY HAZARDOUS FOODS

Examples of potentially hazardous foods include but are not limited to meats, fish, milk, creamed beef, gravies, soups, and chicken. Extra care and precautions must be taken with these potentially hazardous foods. Five factors most often involved in outbreaks of diarrhea caused by contaminated foods are—

- Failing to keep potentially hazardous foods cold (below 40° F) or hot (above 140° F).

- Allowing potentially hazardous foods to remain at warm temperatures (41° F to 139° F).

- Preparing foods 3 hours or more before being served.

- Allowing sick employees to work.

- Permitting poor personal hygiene or sanitation practices by food handlers. Example: Not washing hands after using the latrine; improperly washing and sanitizing all cooking utensils.

STEPS OF PERFORMANCE:

IN GARRISON OR WHEN FOOD IS PREPARED IN A FIELD FOOD SERVICE FACILITY:

STEP 1: Have the supervisor check the temperature of potentially hazardous foods.

- If hot—food should be 140° F or above.

- If cold—food should be 40° F or below.

STEP 2: Check personnel for illness and skin infection.

STEP 3: Check food handling techniques and personal hygiene.

STEP 4: Have the supervisor check the food temperature in cold storage units.

STEP 5: Check handwashing facilities. Are they being used by food handlers?

STEP 6: Check doors and windows. Are they closed or screened to prevent flies from entering?

NOTE

See FM 10-23 for the correct operating procedures for a field kitchen facility (mobile field kitchen [MKT-75] or kitchen tent [M-1948]).

WHEN FOOD IS BROUGHT TO YOUR UNIT IN THE FIELD:

STEP 1: Check the preparation of insulated containers.

- For hot foods, the container should be preheated by the use of boiling water. Foods should be placed in the container while they are hot (above 140° F).

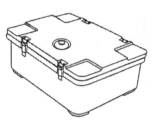

- For cold foods, the container should be prechilled by the use of ice. Foods placed in the container should be cooler than 40° F. Always check the container and the insert seals to ensure that they are intact and in good condition to aid in keeping food at its required temperature.

NOTE

See FM 8-34 and FM 10-23 for the correct procedures for preparing the insulated containers.

STEP 2: When the insulated container arrives, the supervisor must check the food temperature before serving. Make sure it is 140° F or above for hot foods and 40° F or below for cold foods. If the temperature is in the danger zone, contact the medical authority for instructions.

STEP 3: Check for handwashing devices for use by service members.

STEP 4: Check the mess kit laundry, if used. Make sure service members are using the mess kit laundry correctly. The food waste is placed in a scrap can. Wash the kit in warm, soapy water (120° F to 140° F) using a long-handled brush to scrub. Rinse the mess kit in clear, boiling water. Disinfect the mess kit by immersing it in clear, boiling water for 10 seconds. Each mess kit laundry setup of four cans will support 80 personnel. Air-dry mess kits.

NOTE

If a sanitation center or immersion heaters are not available, food service disinfectant may be used. Make sure the label directions are being followed. Each setup of four cans will support 100 personnel. The setup consists of one can for food scraps, one can with soapy water, a clear rinse can, and a final rinse can with food service disinfectant.

STEP 5: Check the sanitation center, if used. The sanitation center is a set of one garbage can and three sinks with the M2 field range burners, or the

modern burner unit, and thermometers. The first sink has warm, soapy water. The second sink has clear, 170° F water. The third sink has clear, 180° F water. If thermometers are not available, the third sink must have boiling water. Food is scraped into the garbage can.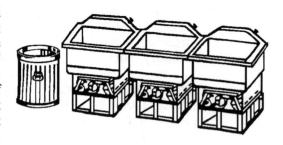
Scrub mess kit in the warm, soapy water by using a long-handled brush. Rinse the mess kit in the second sink of clear, 170° F water. Disinfect the mess kit by immersing it in the third sink of 180° F water for 10 seconds. Air-dry mess kits.

TASK 6: Inspect water containers.

EQUIPMENT NEEDED: None.

WHEN TO INSPECT WATER CONTAINERS:

- Quarterly in garrison when not being used.

- Prior to deployment.

- Before filling at water distribution points.

- Upon completion of use to ensure that all water has been drained from the container before storage.

STEPS OF PERFORMANCE:

UNIT WATER TRAILER:

- Upon completion of use:

  STEP 1: Drain plug and spigots: Make sure that the drain plug has been removed and that all spigots have been opened to drain all water from the tank. Foul odors, bacteria growth, and rust will accumulate during storage if the water is not completely drained.

  STEP 2: Manhole cover: Place a thin piece of wood under the manhole cover to provide ventilation. With the manhole cover and spigots open, air circulation will be allowed, thus drying the inside of the water trailer.

NOTE

See the technical manual on your water trailer for additional guidance.

- Quarterly:

    STEP 1: Manhole cover: Ensure the sealing gasket is in place, free of excessive cracks and dry rot. Cover should provide an effective seal.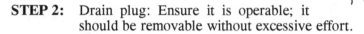

    STEP 2: Drain plug: Ensure it is operable; it should be removable without excessive effort.

    STEP 3: Interior: Check surface for excessive cracks; check for signs of being used for storage of products other than water such as oil products, gasoline, or diesel fuel. Rust stains and other discoloration caused by common natural chemicals in water (iron or manganese) pose no health problem.

    STEP 4: Spigots: Make sure spigots are clean and operable. Covers over spigots should open and close with ease. Spigot handles should operate freely.

NOTE

Questions concerning excessive interior cracks or chipping and use after storage of products other than water should be directed to PVNTMED personnel. Refer to the technical manual on your water trailer for maintenance instructions.

- Before filling at water distribution points:

    STEP 1: Check interior for gross contamination.

    STEP 2: Check hose used to fill trailer. Water point fill hose should not come in contact with the ground. If the hose is lying on the ground, wash the end before use.

    STEP 3: After filling, check manhole cover and drain plug to ensure that they are secure.

CAUTION

Personnel detailed to fill water trailers must be directed to fill the trailers only at approved water points.

COLLAPSIBLE FABRIC DRUMS/PILLOWS/ONION TANKS:

STEP 1: Interior: Check for dirt and other contamination; check for holes.

STEP 2: Fill holes: Check to ensure that fill holes are clean and covers are in place.

STEP 3: Exterior: Check to ensure the exterior is free of oils and other contaminants that may seep into the bag and contaminate the water.

LYSTER BAGS:

STEP 1: Interior: Check for dirt and other contamination; check for holes.

STEP 2: Cover: Check to make sure it fits. Check for holes.

STEP 3: Spigots: Make sure spigots are clean and in place.

STEP 4: Location: Elevate Lyster bags sufficiently to prevent contamination of spigots by wildlife.

NOTE

Always clean the Lyster bag prior to its first use and periodically thereafter with potable water.

WATER CANS: Check interior for contamination; if can has a fuel odor, such as gasoline, do not use it for drinking water.

TASK 7: Check unit water supply for chlorine residual.

EQUIPMENT NEEDED: Field chlorination kit containing chlorine ampules, color comparator, and chlorine test tablets.

Check the chlorine residual when—

- Filling unit containers at water distribution points.

- Water containers arrive in unit area.

- Directed by command medical authority.

- Treating a raw water supply.

STEPS OF PERFORMANCE:

STEP 1: Determine the desired chlorine residual in milligrams per liter (mg/L).

- At the point of consumption, water obtained from an approved water distribution point should have at least a trace of chlorine residual.

- When the unit must obtain water from a raw water supply, or from another source such as a stream or pond, the finished product should have a 5-mg/L chlorine residual after 30 minutes. Under certain conditions, the local medical authority may direct a higher residual.

STEP 2: Flush the spigots of the water container being checked and fill the color comparator tube to a point just below the top of the tube.

STEP 3: Place one chlorine test tablet in the comparator and allow it to dissolve.

STEP 4: Hold the color comparator at eye level and toward a good light source.

STEP 5: Compare the color of the water with the color disc on the opposite side of the color comparator.

- The water is safe to use if the color of the water is the same shade or darker than the required color for the chlorine residual.

- The water must be chlorinated if the color is lighter than the required residual.

TASK 8: Chlorinate water supplies.

EQUIPMENT NEEDED: Field chlorination kit, a 6-ounce jar of calcium hypochlorite (HTH) (70 percent chlorine), or a container of 5- to 6-percent household bleach. Chlorinate the water when—

- The water supply has no chlorine residual.

- The chlorine residual is below required level.

- A raw (untreated) or unapproved water supply must be used.

STEPS OF PERFORMANCE:

STEP 1: Before adding chlorine, check the chlorine residual following the procedures in Task 7.

STEP 2: If the chlorine residual is less than the desired level, add enough chlorine to raise the residual to the required level. Use Table A-1 to determine the amount to add to untreated water. If a 10 mg/L chlorine residual is required, double these amounts. To increase the residual in treated water, smaller quantities of chlorine will be needed.

STEP 3: Wait 10 minutes, then check the chlorine residual.

STEP 4: If the residual is less than 5 mg/L, repeat steps 2 and 3 using a smaller amount of chlorine.

STEP 5: If the residual is at least 5 mg/L, wait an additional 20 minutes before drinking.

Table A-1. Amounts of HTH and Bleach Equivalent to a 5 mg/L Dose in Various Volumes of Water Volume*

VOLUME	AMPULES	HTH		5% BLEACH	
		MRE SPOON	MESSKIT SPOON	MRE SPOON	MESSKIT SPOON
5 GAL	0.5			0.5	
10 GAL	1.0			1.0	
20 GAL	1.0			2.0	
32 GAL	2.0			2.0	1.0
36 GAL	2.0	0.5		3.0	1.0
50 GAL	3.0	0.5		3.0	1.0
55 GAL	3.0	0.5		4.0	1.0
100 GAL	6.0	1.0		7.0	2.0
150 GAL	8.0	1.0		10.0	3.0
160 GAL	9.0	1.0		11.0	3.0
250 GAL	14.0	2.0	0.5	17.0	5.0
400 GAL	22.0	3.0	1.0	26.0	7.0
500 GAL	27.0	3.0	1.0	33.0	9.0
1000 GAL	54.0	7.0	2.0	66.0	18.0
3000 GAL	162.0	20.0	6.0	196.0	54.0
5000 GAL	270.0	33.0	10.0	327.0	90.0

* THE QUANTITIES DEPICTED IN THIS TABLE ARE GENERAL GUIDELINES, ACTUAL AMOUNTS MAY VARY BASED ON WATER QUALITY.

TASK 9: Set up, construct, and maintain field waste disposal devices.

EQUIPMENT NEEDED:

- Set up required number of chemical toilets.

- Collect material for type of improvised facilities to be constructed, if required.

- Establish a detail to set up or construct the devices.

DISPOSAL METHODS THAT MAY BE USED IN THE FIELD:

NOTE

Local, state, federal, and host-nation regulations or laws may prohibit burning or burial of waste. The garbage, rubbish, and other such material may have to be transported to a waste disposal facility. Chemical toilets are the required human waste disposal devices for use during field exercises or missions. Improvised devices may be used under emergency conditions; the burn-out latrine is the preferred method for improvised devices.

- Garbage/rubbish disposal.

  - Collect and transport to approved disposal facilities.

- Expedient devices.

  - Burial—Less than 1 week.

  - Incineration—Longer than a week.

- Liquid kitchen or bathing waste disposal.

  - Grease trap.

  - Soakage pits.

  - Evaporation beds.

- Human waste disposal.

- Chemical toilets. Urinals should be provided in these facilities to prevent soiling the toilet seats, if possible.

  - Individual waste collection bags on the march or for small groups in isolated areas.

  - Cat-hole latrine for marches if individual waste collection bags are not available.

- Field expedients when individual waste collection bags are not available—

  - Burn-out latrine.

  - Pail latrine when chemical toilets are not available, the ground is too hard, or the water table is too high (soil is very wet).

  - Straddle trench for 1 to 3 day bivouac sites when burn-out or pail latrine are not available.

  - Deep pit latrine for temporary camps.

  - Soakage pits for urinals at temporary camps.

  - Trough urinal.

  - Pipe urinal.

  - Urinoil. (See page A-44 for further information on the urinoil.)

STEPS OF PERFORMANCE:

  STEP 1: Use the following chart to determine disposal requirements.

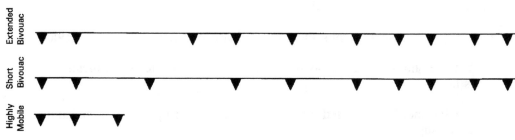

| Highly Mobile | Short Bivouac | Extended Bivouac |

INDIVIDUAL WASTE COLLECTION BAGS
Dispose of with regular waste.

CHEMICAL TOILETS
The preferred field device. Add urinals to protect seats in latrines.

CAT-HOLE
Cover with dirt after use.

STRADDLE TRENCH
Enough for 6 percent of the soldiers.
Cover with dirt after each use.

DEEP PIT
Enough for 6 percent of the soldiers.
Add urinals to protect seats in male latrines.

GARBAGE PIT
Locate near dining facility, but not closer than 100 feet.
One pit per 100 soldiers served per day.
Cover with dirt after each meal; close daily.

SOAKAGE PITS (FOOD SERVICE)
Locate near dining facility; need at least two.
Fill with loose rocks.
Add grease trap for dining facility waste.
Alternate daily use.

SOAKAGE PIT (OTHER)
Provide soakage pit for urinals, shower, Lyster bag, or other locations where water collects.

MESS KIT LAUNDRY/SANITATION CENTER
Dig soakage pit to provide good drainage.

HANDWASHING DEVICES
Dig shallow soakage pit.
Collocate with latrines and food facilities.

SHOWERS
Dig soakage pit.

URINALS
Trough
Pipe
Urinoil

A-35

STEP 2: Select site of construction.

- Garbage and soakage pits should be at least 30 meters from food service.

- Latrine should be as far as possible from food service (100 meters or more is best).

- Latrine should be located on level ground. Never uphill from the campsite or water supplies.

STEP 3: Construct disposal facility.

- **Garbage pit**—Used to prevent accumulation of garbage in the unit area.

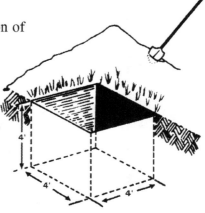

NOTE

Garbage and rubbish should be transported to an approved landfill or must be buried or burned. If buried for short stays, cover daily. For longer periods, garbage and rubbish may have to be burned; however, the ashes should be buried. (Reader should consult the note on page A-32.)

• **Soakage pit/trench**—Used to prevent accumulation of liquid waste (water from showers, sinks, and field kitchens).

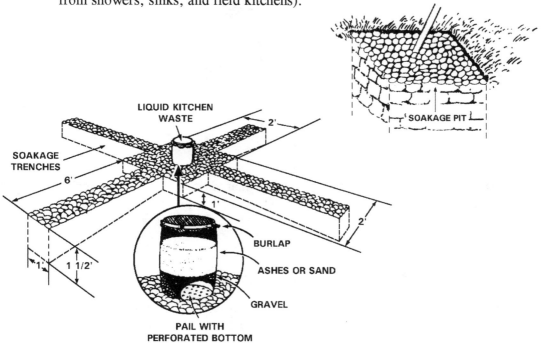

- **Grease trap**—Used with both soakage pit and trench to prevent clogging of soil.

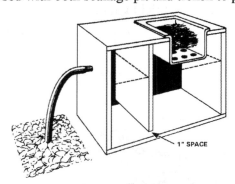

- **Cat-hole latrine**—Used only on the march (if individual waste collection bags are not available) and covered immediately after use.

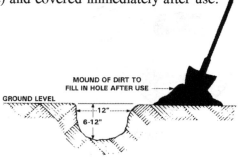

• **Chemical toilets**—Used as the standard field latrine.

BRIEF RELIEF (INDIVIDUAL)

DISPOSA-JOHN

INDIVIDUAL SERVICE MEMBER FIELD TOILET

DROP-BOX TOILET

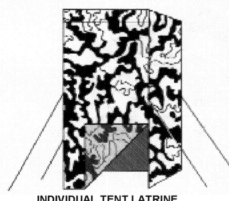

INDIVIDUAL TENT LATRINE

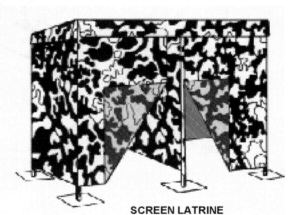

SCREEN LATRINE

A-39

• **Straddle trench latrine**—Used on short bivouacs and field training exercises. Two trenches per 100 males and three trenches per 100 females.

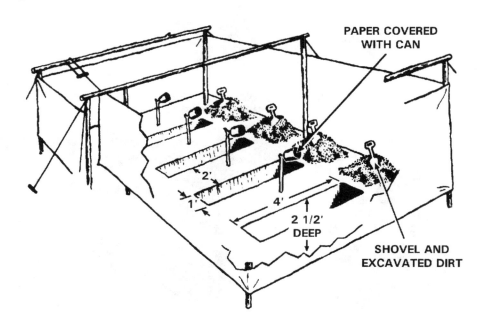

• **Deep pit latrine**—Used for longer periods of time and in built-up areas. Collapsible two-seat boxes are available in the supply system.

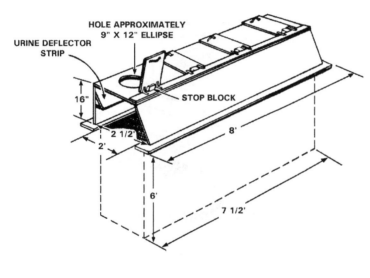

NOTE

If ground is too hard for digging, or if the water table is too high, use a pail latrine or a burn-out latrine.

- **Pail latrine**—Use where water table is too close to the surface of the ground for digging a deep pit latrine.

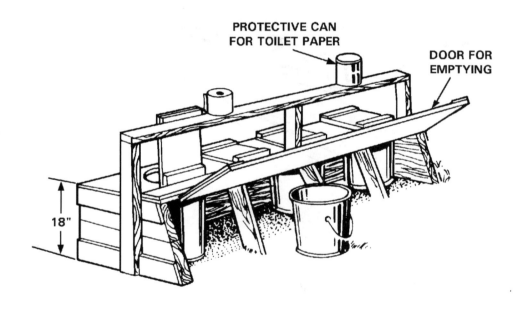

- **Burn-out latrine**—Use where water table is too close to the surface of the ground for digging a pit latrine, or stay is for an extended period.

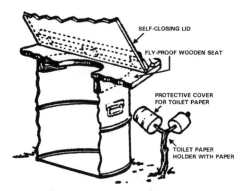

SELF-CLOSING LID

FLY-PROOF WOODEN SEAT

PROTECTIVE COVER FOR TOILET PAPER

TOILET PAPER HOLDER WITH PAPER

- **Urinals**—For male latrines, construct one of the following urinals: trough urinal, pipe urinal, or urinoil.

10'

1'

TROUGH URINAL

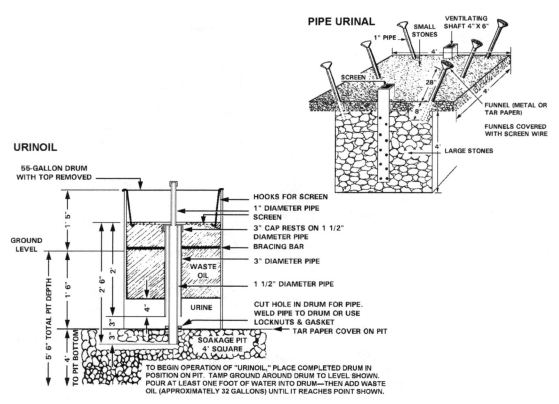

PIPE URINAL

1" PIPE

SMALL STONES

VENTILATING SHAFT 4" X 6"

SCREEN

4'

28"

4'

8"

FUNNEL (METAL OR TAR PAPER)

FUNNELS COVERED WITH SCREEN WIRE

LARGE STONES

4'

URINOIL

55-GALLON DRUM WITH TOP REMOVED

1' 5"

GROUND LEVEL

1' 6"

2' 6"

2'

5' 6" TOTAL PIT DEPTH

4' TO PIT BOTTOM

3"

3"

4"

WASTE OIL

URINE

SOAKAGE PIT 4' SQUARE

HOOKS FOR SCREEN

1" DIAMETER PIPE SCREEN

3" CAP RESTS ON 1 1/2" DIAMETER PIPE

BRACING BAR

3" DIAMETER PIPE

1 1/2" DIAMETER PIPE

CUT HOLE IN DRUM FOR PIPE. WELD PIPE TO DRUM OR USE LOCKNUTS & GASKET

TAR PAPER COVER ON PIT

TO BEGIN OPERATION OF "URINOIL," PLACE COMPLETED DRUM IN POSITION ON PIT. TAMP GROUND AROUND DRUM TO LEVEL SHOWN. POUR AT LEAST ONE FOOT OF WATER INTO DRUM—THEN ADD WASTE OIL (APPROXIMATELY 32 GALLONS) UNTIL IT REACHES POINT SHOWN.

A-44

STEP 4: Inspect daily to make sure that the following is done:

- Waste is collected and transported to an approved disposal facility.

- Straddle trench latrines and garbage pits are covered with dirt daily.

- Pail latrines are emptied and cleaned daily.

- Burn-out latrine containers are rotated and contents burned daily. · Facilities (not the contents) are sprayed with insecticide for fly control when other control techniques fail.

STEP 5: Close improvised latrines and garbage pits when filled to within 1 foot of the ground surface. Have chemical toilet contents removed daily.

Close out by—

- Spraying with residual insecticide.

- Packing earth in successive 3-inch layers until mounded 1 foot above ground level. Spraying again with residual insecticide.

- Posting a sign stating, "Closed latrine/garbage pit and date" (except in combat).

TASK 10:   Construct and maintain field handwashing and shower devices.

EQUIPMENT NEEDED: Personnel detailed to construct and maintain field handwashing and shower devices. Material as required for type of facilities to be constructed.

STEPS OF PERFORMANCE:

    STEP 1:   Select device to be constructed.

      •   Handwashing devices.

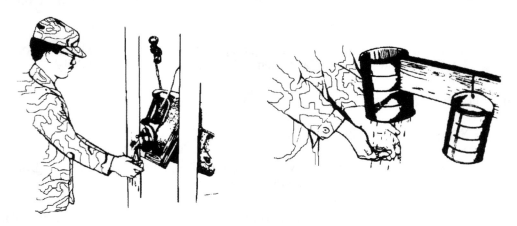

• Shower devices.

STEP 2: Construct devices.

• Collocate handwashing devices at food service and latrine locations.

NOTE

A soakage pit should be provided for all handwashing and shower facilities.

STEP 3: Maintain devices. A supply of soap and water must be available at all times.

STEP 4: Close devices.

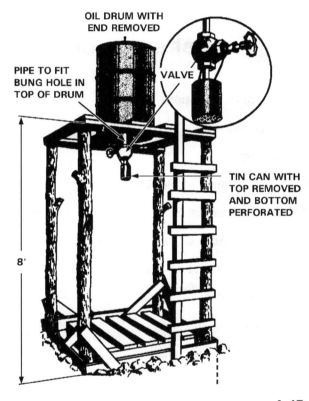

OIL DRUM WITH
END REMOVED

PIPE TO FIT
BUNG HOLE IN
TOP OF DRUM

VALVE

TIN CAN WITH
TOP REMOVED
AND BOTTOM
PERFORATED

8'

GLOSSARY

ABBREVIATIONS AND ACRONYMS

AO   area of operations

attn   attention

C   centigrade

DA   Department of the Army

DEET   75 percent N, N-diethyl-M-Toluamide

DNBI   disease and nonbattle injury

DOD   Department of Defense

F   Fahrenheit

FM   field manual

FST   field sanitation team

gal   gallon

GTA   graphic training aid

hr   hour

HSS   health service support

HTH   calcium hypochlorite, 70 percent available chlorine

lb   pound

LP   listening post

MCRP   Marine Corps Reference Publication

mg/L   milligrams per liter

min   minute

MOPP   mission-oriented protective posture

mph   miles per hour

MRE   meal(s), ready to eat

MSDS   material safety data sheets

NBC nuclear, biological, and chemical

NL no limit

NSN National Stock Number

OP observation post

PMM preventive medicine measures

psi pounds per square inch

PVNTMED preventive medicine

qt quart

SOP standing operating procedure

STD sexually transmitted disease

US United States

UV ultraviolet

WBGT wet bulb globe temperature

REFERENCES

Joint or Multiservice Publications

AR 40-562. *Immunizations and Chemoprophylaxis*. AFJI 48-110; BUDMEDINST 6230.15; CG COMDTINST M6230.4E. 1 November 1995.

FM 8-33. *Control of Communicable Diseases Manual* (16th Edition). NAVMED P-5038. 9 April 1996.

TM 5-632. *Military Entomology Operational Handbook*. NAVFAC MO-310; AFM 9-16. 1 December 1971. (Reprinted with basic including Changes 1—2, January 1976).

TB Med 81. *Cold Injury*. NAVMED P-5052-29; AFP 161-11. 30 September 1976.

TB Med 507. *Occupational and Environmental Health Prevention, Treatment, and Control of Heat Injury*. NAVMED P-5052-5; AFP 160-1. 25 July 1980.

DOD Instruction 4150.7. *DOD Pest Management Program*. 22 April 1996.

Army Publications

AR 40-5. *Preventive Medicine*. 15 October 1990.

AR 40-35. *Preventive Dentistry*. 26 March 1989.

DA Pam 600-63-11. *Dental Health Module for "Fit to Win" Program*. September 1987.

FM 8-34. *Food Sanitation for the Supervisor*. 30 December 1983.

FM 8-250. *Preventive Medicine Specialist*. 27 January 1986. (Reprinted with basic including Change 1, 12 September 1986).

FM 21-10/MCRP 4-11.1D

FM 10-23. *Basic Doctrine for Army Field Feeding and Class I Operations Management.* 18 April 1996.

FM 10-52. *Water Supply in Theaters of Operations.* 11 July 1990.

FM 10-52-1. *Water Supply Point Equipment and Operations.* 18 June 1991.

FM 21-11. *First Aid for Soldiers.* 27 October 1988. (Reprinted with basic including Changes 1—2, 4 December 1991).

FM 21-20. *Physical Fitness Training.* 30 September 1992. (Change 1, 1 October 1998).

FM 21-76. *Survival.* 5 June 1992.

CTA 50-900. *Clothing and Individual Equipment.* 1 September 1994.

TB Med 530. Occupational and Environmental Health Food Service Sanitation. 28 November 1991.

TB Med 561. Occupational and Environmental Health Pest Surveillance. 1 June 1992.

TB Med 577. Occupational and Environmental Health: Sanitary Control and Surveillance of Field Water Supplies. 7 March 1986.

GTA 5-8-12. *Individual Safety Card.* 25 February 1999.

GTA 8-6-12. *Adverse Effects of Cold.* 1 August 1985.

Department of the Defense Form

1532-1. *Pest Management Maintenance Record.* August 1996 (EG).

Technical Notes

United States Army Research Institute of Environmental Medicine, Natick, MA 01760.

USARIEM TN 93-1. Sustaining Soldier Health and Performance in Somalia: Guidance for Small Unit Leaders, December 1992.

USARIEM TN 93-6. Sustaining Soldier Health and Performance in Yugoslavia: Guidance for Small Unit Leaders, June 1993.

USARIEM TN 94-4. Sustaining Soldier Health and Performance in Haiti: Guidance for Small Unit Leaders, September 1994.

USARIEM TN 95-1. Sustaining Soldier Health and Performance in Southwest Asia: Guidance for Small Unit Leaders, October 1995.

INDEX